Michigan Wildflowers

IN COLOR

Revised Edition

Harry C. Lund
Author and Photographer

Holt, Michigan

Published by Thunder Bay Press
2325 Jarco Drive
Holt, Michigan 48842

ISBN: 1-882376-56-0

Library of Congress Cataloging-in-Publication Data

Lund, Harry C.
    Michigan wildflowers : in color / Harry C. Lund,
    author and photographer.—Rev. ed.
    Includes bibliographical references and index.
    ISBN: 1-882376-56-0
1. Wild flowers—Michigan—Identification.
2. Wild flowers—Michigan—Pictorial works.   I. Title

QK167.L86 1998
582. 13'09774—dc21   98-14456
                                                 CIP

Printed in China

Dedicated to my wife, Eloise Eckerman Lund,
with my sincere thanks for all her help and support.

Contents

Foreword

Foreword 4

Introduction 5

Format 6
    Habitats 6
    Nomenclature 7
    Visibility Rating 7

Quick Reference Tables 8

Glossary 15

Flower Photos and Descriptions . . . 18
    White Flowers 24
    Yellow and Orange Flowers 54
    Pink to Red Flowers 72
    Lavender to Purple Flowers 90
    Blue Flowers 98
    Green and Brown Flowers 106

Wildflower Quiz 110

Observer's List 115

Wildflower Trails 123

Index 140

Bibliography 144

Education is the lantern of the soul. How fortunate we in Michigan are to have writers able to produce a book that opens new avenues of learning to children, students, and adults.

The author has spent innumerable days, weeks, and months in search of his subject matter. Flowers have their own time of emergence, often in such simultaneous numbers and of such duration of bloom that years are involved to capture them all photographically. This book is easy enough for any layman to understand, and yet is complete enough in nomenclature to whet the appetite of anyone who has ever wanted to know the name of a wildflower.

This book is the meeting of Michigan's wealth of nature with the searching minds of lovers of the outdoors. Through it may you become more aware of the great need to protect our rich heritage of beauty in Michigan.

Mrs. William B. Heermann (Erie),
President, 1983-1985
The Federated Garden Clubs
of Michigan, Inc.

Introduction

Experience with a former book, *Wildflowers of Sleeping Bear*, indicated that people enjoy wildflower identification by means of color illustrations. It also made clear that a publication of this kind with a broader coverage will fill an often expressed need. Thus, this attempt to present the most common, most interesting, and most visible wildflowers in the state of Michigan is an answer to this need. With but a few exceptions, this publication covers the herbaceous, or non-woody, types of vegetation commonly thought of as wildflowers. It does include a few shrubs and vines that are so showy as to demand inclusion. Also included are plants often thought of as weeds.

Even though 268 species of wildflowers are represented here, it is certain that specimens will be encountered that are not illustrated. In a work of this kind it is a major task to decide which species to include because, unfortunately, a line does have to be drawn. From my own experience there is nothing more frustrating than to find, after much searching, that the flower at hand is not included in the book you have. As with all before me who have written books of this kind, I am sincerely sorry that this has to happen.

Anyone interested in wildflower identification is urged to have and use a good magnifying glass. A hand lens of 10 power magnification is small, inexpensive, convenient, and will not only aid in discerning distinguishing characteristics of plants, but will open up a whole new exciting and interesting world.

As a very general help to identification, a VISIBILITY RATING INDEX is used.

A capital letter at each illustration indicates the visibility rating (see **Visibility Rating Key**). While not precise and very much dependent on the season of the year, the general weather conditions, and the locations within the state, this system hopefully will be helpful, especially in easily locating flowers that form great masses along our roadways.

As everyone recognizes, there are wildflowers that need the help of all of us to keep from vanishing from our heritage. Public Act 182 of 1962 (Christmas Trees, Boughs, Plants and Other Trees) prohibits cutting, removal, transportation, or sale of certain plants without the written permission of the landowner. These plants are designated in this book as **A PROTECTED MICHIGAN WILDFLOWER—DO NOT DISTURB**. Plants without legal protection whose continued existence is precarious are labeled **PLEASE DO NOT PICK**. Those threatened and protected by law according to Public Act 203 of 1974 as amended are labeled **A THREATENED SPECIES—DO NOT DISTURB**. These warnings will be listed below the plant descriptions.

For information on the current protection status of a particular species, contact the Endangered Species Coordinator at the Wildlife Division of the Michigan Department of Natural Resources.

Wildflowers growing on state or national park lands, nature reserves, and other designated areas are not to be disturbed under any circumstances.

So, as the Birders say to each other, "Good Birding," I say to you:

Good Blooming!

Format

The basic organization of flowers in this book is within one of six color groupings: white, yellow and orange, pink to red, lavender to purple, blue, or green and brown. Within each color group an attempt is made to follow a seasonal sequence, with early blooming flowers preceding those coming later. Beyond this basic framework, flowers that are similar or botanically related are placed together where possible.

Each plant description contains the following information in this order:

- Most recognized common name in this area (where a second commonly accepted name is popular, it is also given)
- Technical genus and species name
- Common family name
- Technical family name
- Habitat(s) where commonly found.
- Season of bloom
- Height of plant at blossom time
- Flower description
- Leaf description
- Stem description, if needed for identification
- Description of the fruit, particularly if the fruit is a berry or is berrylike (also, when known, an indication of the fruit's toxicity or edibility)
- Whether the plant grows in groups (colonies)
- An indication as to whether the plant has legal protection as a Protected Michigan Wildflower, an Endangered or Threatened Species, or the informal (nonlegal) protection requested by the Michigan Department of Natural Resources

Habitats

The habitat, or environment, preferred by a plant is placed in one or more of the following:

woods: areas of hardwood (deciduous) trees consisting primarily of beech, birch, soft maple, hard maple, ash or basswood, including the edges of these wooded areas. Wildflowers occurring here are usually the early spring blooming types found before the trees are in full leaf.

dry woods: predominant tree species are aspen (poplar) and oak representing the deciduous trees, and various coniferous (evergreen) trees including white, jack, and red pine. Bracken firs are commonly found.

wet woods: stands of mostly coniferous trees such as black spruce and balsam fir growing on moist sites, and having ground cover of sphagnum and other mosses, ferns and liverworts. Most common in the northern part of the state.

dunes: sandy areas of sparse and scattered vegetation bordering the Great Lakes, particularly the east shore of Lake Michigan. Also includes inland areas of similar characteristics formed on glacier deposited sands or ancient sandy beach ridges. Typical vegetation is juniper, beach grass, scattered pines, sand cherry and other shrubs.

meadows: as used in this book includes most open areas with (usually) no, or very scattered, tree or shrub growth. For example, abandoned farm fields, fence rows, roadsides, ditch-banks, waste areas, and even clearings in the woods. May be dry or moist.

Habitats (cont.)

swamps: low areas with a high water table so there is usually standing stagnant water. Tree growth is primarily white cedar that creates dense shade.

bogs: wet areas of densely matted vegetation formed of various sedges and other water tolerant plants and their decaying parts floating on the edges of some lakes and ponds or adjacent to them. As one walks on these mats they tend to sag and undulate. Their instability requires extreme care on the part of anyone walking on them.

swales: depressions in the terrain, usually limited in area, and wet or moist most of the year. Also includes river and stream bottomlands where pools and puddles are found in the spring.

aquatic: permanently wet areas such as ponds, lakes, and slow flowing streams.

shores: rocky, gravelly, or sandy beaches, particularly those of the Great Lakes, but also includes inland lakes.

Visibility Rating

A capital letter symbol is found adjacent to each illustration. For the few flowers that are not illustrated, the letter is found in the Summary List on pages 8 through 15. The letters have the following meanings:

A Conspicuous flowers readily visible from a moving vehicle at normal highway driving speed. Usually create extensive masses of color.

B Distinctive flowers easily visible from a moving vehicle at normal highway driving speed but very seldom forming extensive masses of color.

C Showy flowers that are harder to find, either because of the nature of the blossoms, the habitats, or the rarity of the plants. Visible mainly along trails and off-road situations.

D Inconspicuous flowers visible to the careful observer.

Nomenclature

The scientific names used are from the *Manual of Vascular Plants of Northeastern United States and Adjacent Canada* by Henry A. Gleason and Arthur Cronquist, 1963. In some instances, the genus-species capitalization has been modernized.

visibility rating	spring	summer	fall	white	yellow-orange	pink-red	lavender-purple	blue	green-brown	GUIDE — Flowers WHITE or predominently WHITE	page	woods	dry woods	wet woods	dunes	meadows	swamps	bogs	swales	aquatic	shores
C	•	•		•						Alyssum, Hoary	44		•			•					
B	•	•		•						Anemone, Canada	28					•			•		
C	•			•		•				Anemone, Rue & False	30	•									
C	•			•		•				Anemone, Wood	28	•									
D	•			•		•				Arbutus, Trailing	28		•								
C		•		•						Asphodel, Sticky False	36							•	•		•
C		•		•			•			Aster, Flat-topped	52					•			•		
D		•		•						Baneberry, Red	40	•									
D		•		•						Baneberry, White	40	•									
C	•	•		•		•				Bearberry	34				•						
C		•		•		•				Bindweed, Field	44				•	•					
C	•			•						Bloodroot	26	•				•		•	•		
B		•	•	•			•			Boneset	50					•		•	•		
D	•	•		•	•		•			Broom-rape, Clustered	34				•						
D	•	•		•		•				Buckbean	34							•	•		•
C	•	•		•						Bunchberry	28	•		•		•					
A	•	•		•						Campion, Bladder	36					•					
C		•	•	•						Campion, White	50					•					
A		•	•	•						Carrot, Wild	44					•					
C	•	•	•	•		•	•			Catnip	32					•					
C		•	•	•						Chamomile, Scentless	38					•					
D	•	•		•						Cinquefoil, Three-toothed	36										•
C		•		•						Comandra, Northern	40			•				•			•
D		•		•						Cow Wheat	48	•						•			•
C		•	•	•						Cucumber, Wild	52	•								•	
B		•		•		•				Culver's Root	48					•					
A		•		•						Daisy, Ox-eye	42					•					
C	•	•	•	•						Dogfennel	38					•					
C	•			•						Dutchman's Breeches	26	•									
A		•		•						Everlasting, Pearly	42					•					
A	•	•	•	•		•				Fleabane	36					•					
C	•			•						Foamflower	26	•									
D	•			•						Ginseng, Dwarf	32	•				•					
D	•			•						Goldthread	24			•				•	•		
C		•	•	•						Grass-of-Parnassus	52					•	•	•	•		•
C	•	•		•						Grass-of-Parnassus, Small	52					•	•	•	•		•
D	•	•		•					•	Greenbrier	34			•					•		
C		•	•	•						Hemlock, Water-	44					•	•				
D		•	•	•						Indian Pipe	48	•						•			
C		•		•			•			Indigo, Prairie False	38	•				•					

visibility rating	season of bloom			flower color						Guide (cont.) — Flowers WHITE or predominently WHITE (cont.)	page	habitats									
	spring	summer	fall	white	yellow-orange	pink-red	lavender-purple	blue	green-brown			woods	dry woods	wet woods	dunes	meadows	swamps	bogs	swales	aquatic	shores
D		•	•	•						Ladies'-tresses, Common	50					•		•	•		
C		•	•	•	•				•	Lettuce, White	52	•									
D		•		•						Lily, Dune	44				•						•
D	•			•						Lily, Fawn	54	•							•		
C	•			•						Lily-of-the-valley, Wild	26	•							•		
B		•		•		•				Mallow, Musk	82					•					
C	•			•						May Apple	30	•									
A		•		•					•	Meadow-rue, Purple	42					•	•		•		•
B		•		•		•				Meadowsweet	40					•			•		
C	•			•						Mitrewort	24	•									
D	•	•		•						Mitrewort, Naked	24						•	•			
C		•	•	•	•		•			Mullein, Moth	40					•					
C		•		•						Nightshade, Enchanter's	34	•									
C		•		•	•					Painted Cup, Pale	48	•									•
B		•		•						Parsnip, Cow	44					•			•		
C		•		•						Parsnip, Water	46					•	•		•		
D		•		•						Partridgeberry	42	•	•								
D		•		•						Poison Ivy	48	•	•		•	•					
D	•			•		•	•			Primrose, Birdseye	28										•
C	•	•		•						Rock Cress, Lyre-leaved	32					•					•
C		•		•						Sandwort, Rock	38				•						•
D	•			•						Sarsaparilla	32	•									
D		•		•						Sarsaparilla, Bristly	32		•		•						
C		•		•						Shinleaf	46	•									
D		•		•					•	Shinleaf, Green	46		•								
D		•		•					•	Sidebells	46	•						•			
D	•	•		•						Snakeroot, Black	36	•									
C		•	•	•						Snakeroot, White	42	•									
C	•	•		•						Solomon's Seal, False	38	•									
D	•	•		•						Solomon's Seal, Hairy	38	•									
D	•	•		•						Solomon's Seal, Smooth	38	•									
C	•	•		•						Solomon's Seal, Starry False	38	•			•						
C	•			•						Spring Cress	24	•								•	
B		•	•	•						Spurge, Flowering	32		•			•					
C	•			•						Squirrel Corn	26	•									
C	•	•		•						Starflower	26	•						•	•		
D	•			•						Starwort	34		•		•						
D	•			•						Stichwort, Lesser	34	•				•					
C	•	•		•						Strawberry, Wild	36					•					
D	•	•		•						Strawberry, Woodland	36	•				•					

visibility rating	spring	summer	fall	white	yellow-orange	pink-red	lavender-purple	blue	green-brown	Guide (cont.)	page	woods	dry woods	wet woods	dunes	meadows	swamps	bogs	swales	aquatic	shores
										Flowers WHITE or predominently WHITE (cont.)											
D		●		●		●				Sundew, Round-leaved	50						●	●			
D	●			●						Sweet Cicely	30	●									
B		●		●						Thimbleberry	40	●				●					
D	●	●	●	●	●					Thistle, Pitcher's	32				●						
C	●	●		●						Toadflax, Bastard	40		●			●					
C	●			●		●				Toothwort, Broadleaf	24	●							●		
C	●			●		●				Toothwort, Cutleaf	24	●							●		
B	●			●		●				Trillium	30	●									
D	●	●		●						Trillium, Nodding	30	●									
B		●	●	●		●	●			Turtlehead	48					●			●		
C	●	●		●				●	●	Violet, Canada	30	●									
B		●	●	●						Virgin's Bower	52	●							●		
C	●			●						Water Arum	28						●	●		●	
D		●	●	●						Water-horehound, Cut-leaf	50						●		●		
B		●		●						Water Lily, White	50									●	
D		●		●						Wintergreen	46		●								
D		●		●		●				Woodnymph	46						●	●	●		
A		●	●	●		●				Yarrow	52					●					
										Flowers YELLOW and ORANGE											
C		●			●					Agrimony	66	●	●			●		●			
C	●				●					Bellwort, Large-flowered	54	●									
A		●	●		●					Birdsfoot Trefoil	68					●					
A		●	●		●					Black-eyed Susan	64					●					
A		●	●		●					Butter-and-eggs	68					●					
B	●	●	●		●					Buttercup	54					●	●		●		
B		●	●		●	●				Butterfly Weed	62				●	●					
C		●	●		●					Cherry, Ground	68					●					
B		●			●					Cinquefoil, Sulfur	64					●					
C	●	●			●					Clintonia	54	●						●			
B		●	●		●					Coneflower, Tall	70					●	●				
A	●	●			●					Coreopsis	56		●		●	●					
D	●				●					Cucumber-root, Indian	54	●									
A	●	●	●		●					Dandelion, Common	56					●					
B		●	●		●		●			Goat's-beard	62					●					
C		●			●	●				Goat's Rue	56		●			●					
C	●	●			●					Golden Alexanders	60					●			●		
C		●	●		●					Goldenrod, Bluestem	70	●	●			●					●
A		●	●		●					Goldenrod, Canada	70					●					

visibility rating	spring	summer	fall	white	yellow-orange	pink-red	lavender-purple	blue	green-brown	Guide (cont.) Flowers YELLOW and ORANGE (Cont.)	page	woods	dry woods	wet woods	dunes	meadows	swamps	bogs	swales	aquatic	shores
A	●	●			●					Hawkweed, Field or Yellow	60					●					
A		●	●		●	●				Hawkweed, Orange	64					●					
A		●			●					Hawkweed, Smoothish	60					●					
C	●	●			●					Heather, False	58				●						
D		●	●	●	●		●			Horsemint	68				●	●					
C		●	●		●					Jewelweed, Spotted	64					●			●		
C		●			●					King Devil	60					●					
C	●				●					Lady's-slipper, Yellow	58			●			●	●			
B	●	●			●					Lily, Day	62					●			●		
B		●			●	●				Lily, Michigan	62					●			●		
B		●			●	●				Lily, Wood	62				●	●					
C	●				●					Lily, Yellow Trout	54	●		●		●			●		
D	●	●			●					Loosestrife, Tufted	56					●			●		
B	●				●					Marsh Marigold	54						●		●	●	
D	●				●		●			Meadow-rue, Early	42	●							●		
D		●			●					Moneywort	64					●			●		
B		●	●		●					Mullein, Common	68					●					
A	●	●	●		●					Parsnip, Wild	60					●					
D	●				●					Pimpernel, Yellow	60	●				●					
D		●	●		●	●			●	Pinesap	68	●									
B		●			●					Pondlily, Yellow	66									●	
B		●			●					Primrose, Evening	66		●		●	●					
C	●	●			●					Puccoon, Hairy	58		●		●	●					●
C	●	●			●					Puccoon, Hoary	58		●		●	●					●
B	●	●			●					Ragwort, Golden	56						●		●		
A		●	●		●					St. John's-wort, Common	66					●	●		●		●
C		●			●					Silverweed	64					●					●
B		●	●		●					Sowthistle, Smooth	66					●					
B	●	●	●		●					Spurge, Leafy	62				●	●					
D	●				●					Squawroot	58		●								
B		●	●		●					Sunflower, Tall	70					●	●				
B		●	●		●					Sunflower, Woodland	70	●				●			●		
B		●	●		●					Swamp Candle	66			●		●	●		●		
A		●	●		●					Tansy, Common	70					●					
C		●			●					Tansy, Huron	70				●				●		●
C	●		●		●					Violet, Downy Yellow	56	●									
C	●		●		●					Violet, Smooth Yellow	56	●									
C	●				●	●				Wood Betony	58	●	●								
C	●	●	●		●					Wood-sorrel, Yellow	58					●					
A	●	●			●					Yellow Rocket	60					●					

visibility rating	season of bloom			flower color						Guide (cont.) Flowers PINK and RED	page	habitats									
	spring	summer	fall	white	yellow-orange	pink-red	lavender-purple	blue	green-brown			woods	dry woods	wet woods	dunes	meadows	swamps	bogs	swales	aquatic	shores
D	•	•				•				Arethusa	75						•	•			
C		•	•			•	•			Basil, Wild	82	•				•					
B		•				•	•			Bergamot, Wild	82					•					
B		•	•	•		•				Bouncing Bet	86					•					
D		•	•			•	•			Calypso	74			•		•					
B		•	•	•		•				Cardinal-flower	88					•				•	
B	•	•	•			•				Clover, Red	80					•					
C	•	•				•				Columbine	72	•	•								
C		•				•				Corn Cockle	86					•					
D	•	•	•			•				Corydalis, Pale	76					•					•
D		•				•				Cranberry, Large	80						•	•			
D		•				•				Cranberry, Small	80						•	•			
B	•	•		•		•	•			Dame's Rocket	82	•				•					
C		•		•		•				Dogbane, Spreading	84	•	•			•			•		
A		•	•			•	•			Fireweed	84					•			•		•
C	•	•		•		•				Geranium, Wild	76	•				•			•		
C		•				•	•			Grass Pink	78						•	•	•		
C	•			•		•	•	•		Hepatica, Round-lobed	72	•	•								
C	•			•		•	•	•		Hepatica, Sharp-lobed	72	•	•								
C	•	•				•				Herb-Robert	76	•				•			•		
C	•			•		•	•			Honesty	82	•				•					
A		•	•			•	•			Joe Pye Weed	88						•	•			•
C		•	•			•	•			Knapweed, Brown	88					•					
A		•	•	•		•	•			Knapweed, Spotted	88					•					
C	•	•				•				Lady's-slipper, Pink	74		•				•	•			
D	•			•		•	•			Lady's-slipper, Ram's-head	74	•		•			•	•			•
C		•		•		•				Lady's-slipper, Showy	78			•			•	•			
B		•		•		•				Mallow, Musk	82					•					
B		•				•	•			Milkweed, Common	84				•	•					
B		•		•		•	•			Milkweed, Swamp	84					•	•			•	
C		•		•		•	•		•	Milkwort, Field	84					•	•			•	
C		•		•		•				Milkwort, Racemed	78		•			•					
C		•		•		•				Mullein-pink	86					•					
D	•			•		•	•			Orchis, Showy	74	•				•					
B	•	•	•		•	•				Paintbrush, Indian	72					•					•
C		•				•	•			Pea, Beach	80				•						•
A	•	•		•		•	•			Pea, Everlasting	78					•					
C		•				•				Pink, Deptford	86					•					
D		•		•		•				Pipsissewa	80		•								
C	•	•				•				Pitcher Plant	76						•	•			•

visibility rating	spring	summer	fall	white	yellow-orange	pink-red	lavender-purple	blue	green-brown	Guide (cont.) Flowers PINK and RED (Cont.)	page	woods	dry woods	wet woods	dunes	meadows	swamps	bogs	swales	aquatic	shores
D		•				•				Pogonia, Rose	74						•	•			
C	•	•				•	•			Polygala, Fringed	78	•						•			
D		•				•	•			Pyrola, Pink	80	•						•			
C		•				•				Rose, Smooth	86	•			•	•					
C		•				•				Rose, Swamp	86						•	•	•		
C		•		•		•				Sleepy Catchfly	86		•			•					
C	•					•				Spring Beauty	72	•									
C	•					•				Spring Beauty, Broadleaf	72	•									
B		•	•	•		•	•			Teasel	84					•			•		
B		•	•			•	•			Thistle, Bull	88					•					
B		•	•	•		•	•			Thistle, Canada	88					•			•		
D		•				•	•			Thyme, Wild	82		•			•					•
C		•				•	•			Tick-trefoil, Pointed Leaved	94		•								
C	•			•	•	•	•		•	Trillium, Red	76	•									
D		•				•				Twinflower	78		•	•			•	•			
D	•	•				•	•			Twisted-stalk, Rose	76	•									
D	•	•		•		•	•			Twisted-stalk, White	76	•									
B		•		•		•				Vetch, Crown	80					•					
D	•	•		•	•	•	•			Windflower, Red	72				•						

Flowers LAVENDER to PURPLE

visibility rating	spring	summer	fall	white	yellow-orange	pink-red	lavender-purple	blue	green-brown	Guide	page	woods	dry woods	wet woods	dunes	meadows	swamps	bogs	swales	aquatic	shores
C		•		•			•			Aster, Large-leaved	94	•	•								
B		•	•	•			•	•		Aster, New England	94					•			•		
B		•	•	•			•	•		Aster, Smooth	94				•	•					
C		•					•			Beard-tongue, Hairy	96	•				•					
B		•				•	•			Blazing Star, Rough	94					•					
C		•	•			•	•			Burdock, Common	94					•					
C		•	•			•	•			Burdock, Great	94					•					
C		•					•			Butterwort	92							•			•
C		•					•			Cinquefoil, Marsh	96						•	•	•	•	
D	•				•		•		•	Cohosh, Blue	90	•									
D	•			•	•					Coralroot, Northern or Early	92			•			•				
C		•				•	•			Coralroot, Spotted	92	•	•								
C	•	•				•	•			Coralroot, Striped	92	•	•	•							
D	•					•	•		•	Ginger, Wild	90	•									
C		•	•				•			Goat's-beard, Purple	62					•				•	
C		•				•	•			Hound's Tongue	92				•	•					
D	•						•		•	Jack-in-the-pulpit	90	•						•	•		
A		•	•				•			Loosestrife, Purple	96					•	•			•	•

visibility rating	spring	summer	fall	white	yellow-orange	pink-red	lavender-purple	blue	green-brown	Guide (cont.) — Flowers LAVENDER to PURPLE (Cont.)	page	woods	dry woods	wet woods	dunes	meadows	swamps	bogs	swales	aquatic	shores
D		●	●	●			●			Mint, Wild	98					●					
C		●	●	●		●	●	●		Monkey Flower, Square-stemmed	96						●	●	●		
D		●		●			●			Motherwort	98	●							●		
C		●	●				●	●		Nightshade	96						●		●		
C		●		●		●	●	●		Orchid, Purple Fringed	98					●	●		●		
C		●	●				●	●		Peppermint	98					●			●		
B	●	●					●	●		Phlox, Wood	90	●									
C	●	●	●	●			●	●		Self-heal	92					●					
C		●	●				●	●		Spearmint	98					●			●		
B		●					●			Thistle, Marsh	96					●			●		
B	●	●					●	●		Vetch, Hairy	90					●					
C	●						●	●		Violet, Bird-foot	90		●								
C		●		●			●			Waterleaf, Virginia	92	●							●		

Flowers BLUE

visibility rating	spring	summer	fall	white	yellow-orange	pink-red	lavender-purple	blue	green-brown	Name	page	woods	dry woods	wet woods	dunes	meadows	swamps	bogs	swales	aquatic	shores
D	●			●				●	●	Blue-eyed Grass	100					●					
C	●			●					●	Blue-eyed Mary	98	●							●		
B		●	●	●		●	●	●		Blueweed	102					●					
B		●	●	●		●	●	●		Chicory	104					●					
C	●	●	●	●		●		●		Forget-me-not	102	●				●	●		●		
C		●	●	●			●	●		Gentian, Closed	104	●				●			●		●
C		●	●	●			●	●		Gentian, Fringed	104	●				●			●		●
C	●	●		●		●		●		Harebell	102		●		●	●					
B	●	●						●		Iris, Blue	100						●		●		
C	●			●			●	●		Iris, Dwarf Lake	100							●			●
C		●	●					●		Lobelia, Great	104					●	●		●		●
B	●	●		●		●	●	●		Lupine	100					●					
B		●		●		●	●	●		Lupine, Garden	100					●					
C	●	●						●		Periwinkle	102	●				●					
C		●	●					●		Pickerelweed	102									●	
D		●	●	●		●	●	●		Skullcap, Common	104					●	●				●
D	●	●	●				●	●		Speedwell, Common	102	●		●		●					
B		●	●				●	●		Vervain, Blue	104					●	●		●		
C	●						●	●		Violet, Common Blue	100	●				●					

Flowers GREEN and BROWN

visibility rating	spring	summer	fall	white	yellow-orange	pink-red	lavender-purple	blue	green-brown	Name	page	woods	dry woods	wet woods	dunes	meadows	swamps	bogs	swales	aquatic	shores
D	●								●	Arrow-grass, Seaside	106						●	●			●
B	●	●							●	Cat-tail, Common	106						●	●	●	●	

visibility rating	season of bloom			flower color						Guide (cont.) Flowers GREEN and BROWN	page	habitats									
	spring	summer	fall	white	yellow-orange	pink-red	lavender-purple	blue	green-brown			woods	dry woods	wet woods	dunes	meadows	swamps	bogs	swales	aquatic	shores
C	•	•							•	Cat-tail, Narrow-leaved	106						•	•	•	•	
D		•	•			•			•	Dock, Curled	106					•					
C		•						•	•	Gentian, Spurred	106			•				•	•		
C		•				•			•	Ground Nut	106									•	•
D		•					•		•	Helleborine	108	•									
D		•							•	Orchid, Tall Northern Bog	108			•			•	•	•		
C		•	•						•	Ragweed	108				•	•					
D	•				•		•		•	Skunk Cabbage	106						•		•		
C	•	•				•	•		•	Spurge, Cypress	108					•					
D		•					•		•	Twayblade, Heartleaf	108			•				•	•		
C		•	•	•					•	Wormwood, Tall	108				•						

Glossary

annual – living for a single growing season

axil – the angle between a leaf or branch and the main axis

bicolored – of two colors

bract – a small, rudimentary or imperfectly developed leaf

calyx – sepals collectively form the calyx

corolla – all the petals of a flower make the corolla

chlorophyll – the green pigment in plants that permits the conversion of light energy to food through photosynthesis

cleft – a deep lobe or cut usually applied to leaf margins

entire – without teeth, serrations, or lobes, as leaf margins

exudate – material that has oozed to the surface, usually of a stem or leaf

head – a dense collection of sessile or nearly sessile flowers as in the Composite family

hybridize – the process by which two plants that differ in one or more basic characteristics produce offspring

lateral – on or arising from the side

linear – a long and narrow organ (leaf) with the sides nearly parallel

midrib – middle vein in a leaf

node – the part of a stem where the leaf, leaves, or secondary branches emerge

"petal" – when the word petal occurs in quotation marks it is not a true petal.

prostrate – extended in a horizontal position; trailing on the ground

recurved – curved backward or downward

rhizome – an elongated underground stem

sac – a pouch within a plant often containing fluid

sepal – one member of the calyx

sessile – refers to a flower or leaf lacking a stalk

stipule – a small, leaf-like appendage at the base of a leafstalk in some plants. Usually found in pairs.

toxic – poisonous

tuber – a modified branch, usually underground and for storage of food

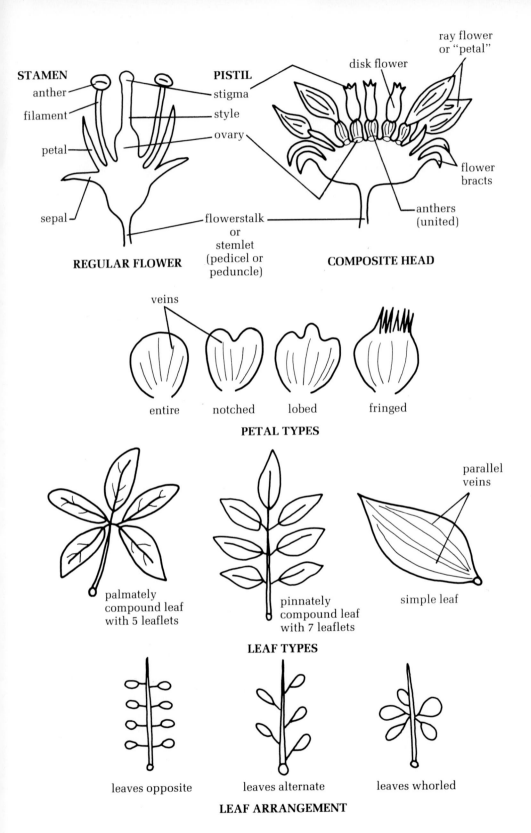

STAMEN
anther
filament
petal
sepal

PISTIL
stigma
style
ovary

flowerstalk
or
stemlet
(pedicel or
peduncle)

REGULAR FLOWER

ray flower
or "petal"
disk flower

flower
bracts

anthers
(united)

COMPOSITE HEAD

veins

entire   notched   lobed   fringed

PETAL TYPES

palmately
compound leaf
with 5 leaflets

pinnately
compound leaf
with 7 leaflets

parallel
veins

simple leaf

LEAF TYPES

leaves opposite   leaves alternate   leaves whorled

LEAF ARRANGEMENT

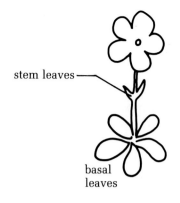

stem leaves

basal leaves

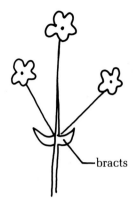

bracts

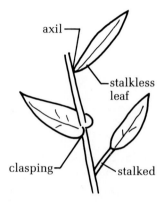

axil

stalkless leaf

clasping

stalked

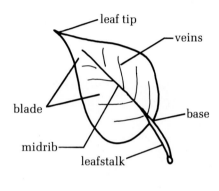

leaf tip

veins

blade

base

midrib

leafstalk

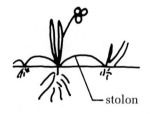

stolon

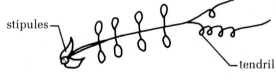

stipules

tendril

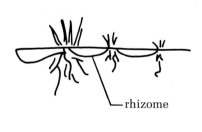

rhizome

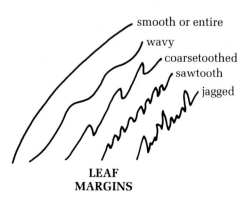

smooth or entire

wavy

coarsetoothed

sawtooth

jagged

LEAF MARGINS

White Flowers

Flowers placed in this section are those ranging from pure white through cream, greenish-white, yellowish-white, and pearly-white.

Also included are those flowers that are basically white but have various colored spots, lines, streaks, or tints.

Pages 24-53

Although found in groups (colonies), Canada Anemone seldom covers extensive areas and therefore is assigned a "B" Visibility Rating.

Yellow and Orange Flowers

Flowers in this section are yellow and orange and include those that are described as greenish-yellow, orange-yellow, yellow-orange, and red-orange.

Pages 54-71

A mixture of Smoothish Hawkweed, Orange Hawkweed, and Ox-Eye Daisy in a meadow habitat along an Upper Peninsula highway. These species all have an "A" Visibility Rating.

Pink to Red Flowers

Includes flowers that are definitely pink to red and also the variations of dusky pink, crimson, and rose. Some bicolored flowers containing pink with some other color are also in this group.

Pages 72-89

The color groupings of "Pink and Red" flowers, "Lavender and Purple" flowers, and "Blue" flowers may be more of a hindrance than a help. Few people would agree on many of the hues, tints, and shades encountered in these colors. So please be patient and if you don't find the flower that to you is certainly pink (for example), try the other color categories.

Cardinal-Flower, a plant of striking beauty from late summer into fall, is given a "B" Visibility Rating because it rarely forms extensive masses of color.

Lavender to Purple Flowers

Includes flowers that are some shade of purple, ranging from lavender to violet, magenta, red-purple, and dark purple.

Pages 90-99

Purple Loosestrife is often found in extensive patches which, along with its bright color ranging from purple to pink, gives it an "A" Visibility Rating. A plant of swales, marshy lake beaches, river banks, and other moist areas.

Blue Flowers

Flowers that are unquestionably blue are placed here, but there are some borderline shades, such as violet-blue.

Pages 98-105

Garden Lupine is an escape from the gardens of the early settlers, and patches of these showy flowers are now found growing wild, particularly in the western Upper Peninsula.

Green and Brown Flowers

Although the flowers in this group are basically green, some of them have parts marked with brown or purple or brownish-purple.

Pages 106-109

Because of their flower color, plants such as Tall Wormwood and the others in this group require close attention to determine that the flowers are present, as they may be casually mistaken for seeds or leaves.

Broadleaf Toothwort

or Pepperwort
Dentaria diphylla Michx.
Mustard family   Cruciferae

woods   spring   8-12 in. (20-30 cm)

Blossoms are formed at tip of stem in a loose, open cluster of 4-petaled flowers. Color is white, changing to pink as the blossoms mature.

A single pair of leaves on the stem, just above the center of the plant, nearly opposite each other. Each divided into 3 broad leaflets that are up to 1 in. (2.5 cm) across and coarsely toothed.

Stem is smooth and unbranched.

Colonies of plants are common.

Cutleaf Toothwort

Dentaria laciniata Muhl.
Mustard family   Cruciferae

woods   spring   8-12 in. (20-30 cm)

Also has 4-petaled white flowers and is similar to *D. diphylla* but has 3 stem leaves, each divided into 3 long, narrow, deeply cleft, sharp pointed leaflets.

Stem is hairy on the upper part.

Spring Cress

Cardamine bulbosa Schreb.
Mustard family   Cruciferae

woods, swales   spring   8-25 in. (2-6 dm)

A cluster of 4-petaled white flowers that may be tinted pink are at the tip of the stem. Stem leaves are alternate, stalkless, margins entire or with a few very coarse teeth or lobes. Basal leaves are long-stalked, round or kidney-shaped.

Stems may be either smooth or fuzzy.

Fruits are erect, narrow, elongated pods with pointed tips.

Mitrewort or Bishop's Cap

Mitella diphylla L.
Saxifrage family   Saxifragaceae

woods   spring   8-18 in. (2-5 dm)

Flowers are small, white, cup-shaped with lacy fringes. There are 5-20 flowers borne singly along the upper 2-6 in. (5-15 cm) of the stem.

Most of the leaves arise from the base of the plant on long stalks. There is also a pair of stalkless, 3-lobed leaves opposite each other about midway on the stem.

Stems are mostly fuzzy, especially below the stem leaves.

Naked Mitrewort

Mitella nuda L.
Saxifrage family   Saxifragaceae

swamps, bogs   spring, summer
2-8 in. (5-20 cm)

Similar to *M. diphylla* but can be distinguished by the following:

1. The entire plant is smaller

2. The flowers are more yellow-green than white

3. The fringes on the petals are more thread-like.

4. The stem leaves are lacking or there may be 1 leaf present but not 2.

5. The basal leaves are smaller, rounder, and indented at the base.

6. The flowers are borne on the upper 1-4 in. (2-10 cm) of the stem.

7. It is usually found in wetter habitats

8. It blooms a little later in the season.

Goldthread

Coptis trifolia (L.) Salisb.
Crowfoot family   Ranunculaceae

bogs, swamps, wet woods   spring
3-6 in. (8-15 cm)

Delicate white flowers on long flowerstalks arising from the base of plant. Sepals appear as petals, 5-7 in number. Petals are club-shaped and inconspicuous. There are many stamens. There is but one flower on each very fine flowerstalk and it usually projects above the leaves.

The palmately compound leaves arise from the base of the plant, leaflets 3 in number, smooth, shiny on upper surface, dark-green, margins round-toothed; remain green all winter.

Broadleaf
Toothwort

C

Mitrewort   C

Cutleaf
Toothwort

C

Naked
Mitrewort

C

Spring
Cress

C

Goldthread   D

Foamflower or False Mitrewort
Tiarella cordifolia L.
Saxifrage family   Saxifragaceae

woods   spring   6-12 in. (15-30 cm)

Delicate white flowers on short stemlets form a somewhat fuzzy central stem. The long, slender, rodlike stamens arise between the petals.

Leaves are only at the base of the plant on long, definitely fuzzy leafstalks.

Blade (wide part) of the leaf is broad, 3-5 lobed, and is indented at the base.

PLEASE DO NOT PICK

Starflower
Trientalis borealis Raf.
Primrose family   Primulaceae
bogs, swamps, woods   late spring, early summer   4-10 in. (1-2.5 dm)

Flowers white with 5-9 but usually 7 sharp pointed petals. Commonly a pair of flowers at the tip of the plant but may vary from 1-4. Flowerstalk thin and wiry. Stamens prominent, same number as petals.

The shiny, long tapered leaves form a single whorl below the flower, 5-10 in number, 2-4 in. (4-10 cm) long; margins mostly smooth. There may be a leaf below the whorl but, if present, is very small.

PLEASE DO NOT PICK

Dutchman's Breeches
Dicentra cucullaria (L.) Berhn.
Fumitory family   Fumariaceae

woods   spring   6-12 in. (15-30 cm)

White, waxy, inflated flowers dangle from the stem like tiny pantaloons.

There are 2 spurs spreading and extending backward (upward) forming the legs of the breeches. Flowers are yellow-tipped.

Leaves are very finely divided, delicate, long-stalked, and arise from the base of the plant.

Wild Lily-of-the-Valley
or Canada Mayflower
Maianthemum canadense Desf.
Lily family   Liliaceae

woods   spring   2-8 in. (5-20 cm)

Small, individual white flowers cluster together at the tip of the stem to form a delicate, sweet-smelling flower head. Each flower has 4 parts (2 petals and 2 petallike sepals) and each has 4 rodlike projecting stamens.

Leaves usually 2 per plant but may be 1 or 3; the heart-shaped base partially surrounds the stem; leaf veins are parallel, each one extending from the base to the tip of the leaf.

Fruit is a cluster of green berries with reddish speckles, turning light red as it matures. Not edible.

PLEASE DO NOT PICK

Bloodroot
Sanguinara canadensis L.
Poppy family   Papaveraceae

moist woods   spring   2-6 in. (5-15 cm)

A single flower that has white petals and yellow rodlike filaments at its center. Petals usually 8 but sometimes 10 and (rarely) as many as 16. Often 4 petals are longer than the others, imparting a square appearance to the blossom. Flowers close in cold or cloudy weather.

Leaves arise from the base of the plant, are rounded in general outline; margin is wavy to coarsely toothed. Blade is up to 4 in. (10 cm) across at flowering time, growing larger, up to 10 in. (2.5 dm) after flowers fade.

Stems are smooth, erect, leafless, and contain a red juice that can cause a rash or blistering of the skin.

Squirrel Corn
Dicentra canadensis (Goldie) Walp.
Fumitory family   Fumariaceae

woods   spring   6-12 in. (15-30 cm)

Similar to *D. cucullaria* but flowers are more heart-shaped with rounded spurs. It tends to bloom a little later so that Squirrel Corn may be at its prime when Dutchman's Breeches are fading. The two are often found growing side by side.

Foamflower

C

Wild lily-of-the-valley C

Bloodroot

C

Starflower C

Dutchman's Breeches

C

Squirrel Corn

C

WOOD ANEMONE
Anemone quinquefolia L.
Crowfoot family   Ranunculaceae

woods   spring   4-8 in. (1-2 dm)

A single flower up to 1 in. (2.5 cm) across at tip of stem; white (may be pinkish on lower surface) without petals but the sepals appear as petals, usually 5-6 in number. A central tuft of white to yellowish stamens is quite noticeable.

Compound leaves are in a whorl, usually 3, midway on stem. Each leaf is composed of 3-5 deeply cleft and coarsely toothed leaflets. There may be a long-stalked leaf from the base of the plant that is similar to the stem leaves. Usually found in colonies.

CANADA ANEMONE
Anemone canadensis L.
Crowfoot family   Ranunculaceae

meadows, swales   spring-early summer
1-2 ft. (3-6 dm)

A single flower borne at the tip of the stem, 1½ in. (2.5-4 cm) across; 5 white "petals" (actually are sepals).

Stem leaves are large, stalkless, deeply cleft, coarsely toothed, sharp pointed, in whorls of 2-3 midway up stem. Basal leaves similar but long-stalked.

Seed head is round, ball-like, covered with spines that have curved, pointed tips. Usually found in colonies.

WATER ARUM or Wild Calla
Calla palustris L.
Arum family   Araceae

swamps, bogs, ponds   spring
6-16 in. (1.5-4 dm)

"Flower" is a showy, white, oval and sharp pointed bract whose base embraces the stem. Within this structure and terminating the stem is the green, fleshy and knobby spike bearing tiny white flowers. "Flowerstalk" is long, leafless, and arises from base of plant, which is usually submerged in water.

Heart-shaped, smooth and shiny leaves with stalks that are about equal to the length of the blades arise from the base of the plant.

TRAILING ARBUTUS
Epigaea repens L.
Heath family   Ericaceae

dry woods   spring   prostrate

Flowers are 5-petaled, white to pale pink, fragrant, formed in clusters, and are usually hidden beneath the dead leaves on the forest floor.

Leaves are oval-shaped, thick and leathery; margins entire.

PROTECTED MICHIGAN WILDFLOWER DO NOT DISTURB

BUNCHBERRY or Dwarf Cornel
Cornus canadensis L.
Dogwood family   Cornaceae

swamps, woods   late spring-summer
8-10 in. (2-2.5 dm)

What appear to be the flowers are 4 white, showy "petals" (actually modified leaves) surrounding the cluster of greenish to cream-colored true flowers in the center.

Leaves are dull green above and shiny below, have prominent and parallel veins, are rounded with pointed tips, and form a whorl or circle of 6 near the top of the plant.

Stems are ridged and woody. Fruit is a cluster of shiny, red berries; not toxic but bland. Usually found in colonies.

BIRDSEYE PRIMROSE
Primula mistassinica Michx.
Primrose family   Primulaceae

rocks, shores   spring
4-10 in. (1-2.5 dm)

Flowers mostly white with a faint pink or lavender tint but occasionally lavender colored flowers are found. The 5 petals each have a notched tip. At the center of the flower is a noticeable yellow circle or "eye." Stamens and pistil are hidden in the tube below the petals. Leaves are ¾-2¾ in. (2-7 cm) long, are oval and tapering to the base, found only as a basal rosette. Margins are smooth to slightly toothed.

Wood
Anemone

C

Trailing Arbutus   D

Canada
Anemone

B

Bunchberry   C

Water
Arum

C

Birdseye Primrose   D

29

TRILLIUM or Large-Flowered Trillium
Trillium grandiflorum (Michx.) Salisb.
Lily family   Liliaceae

woods   spring   12-18 in. (3-5 dm)

Large, white, 3-petaled flowers, 2-3 in. (5-7.5 cm) across, a single flower per stem; 3 prominent, pointed, green sepals below and between the somewhat longer petals.

3 leaves emerge from a single point on the stem (whorl); leaves broad, rapidly narrowing to a pointed tip; leaf veins conspicuous; one set of leaves per plant.

The white flowers turn pink with age. Also, a disease caused by a mycoplasma-like organism results in a green discoloration of the petals ranging from a narrow green streak to a completely green blossom.

**PROTECTED MICHIGAN
WILDFLOWER—DO NOT DISTURB**

MAY APPLE or Mandrake
Podophyllum peltatum L.
Barberry family   Berberidaceae

open woods   spring   12-18 in. (3-5 dm)

Flowers white, fragrant, nodding on short, stout, fuzzy stalks that arise from the fork of the two leaves; one flower per plant. Stamens yellow, rodlike, surround the pistil. The inflated pistil is yellow to yellow-green.

Flowering plants have two deeply lobed leaves that overtop nodding blossom. Immature plants have one umbrella-like leaf.

Fruit is large, lemon shape, edible, not tasty. Plants grow in colonies. Seeds, leaves, and roots are toxic.

RUE ANEMONE
Anemonella thalictroides (L.) Spach.
Crowfoot family   Ranunculaceae

woods   spring   4-10 in. (1-2.5 dm)

5-10 petallike white to pale pink sepals that resemble petals. Flowers about ¾ in. across (2 cm) with 2 or more of them in a loose cluster beneath which is a whorl of blunt-lobed leaflets. Basal leaves long-stalked, each with 3 groups of 3 leaflets, rounded at their base and bluntly lobed at their tips.

FALSE RUE ANEMONE, *Isopyrum biternatum* (Raf.) T.&G. (not shown) is similar in appearance but has smaller flowers (½ in.); leaflets much more deeply lobed at tips.

Flowers usually single. Both species found in southern part of the Lower Peninsula.

NODDING TRILLIUM
Trillium cernuum L.
Lily family   Liliaceae

woods   spring-early summer
6-20 in. (1.5-5 dm)

Similar to *T. grandiflorum*, the most apparent differences being the 3-petaled flower dangles below the leaves on a gently curving flowerstalk and the anthers are pink rather than pale yellow.

**PROTECTED MICHIGAN
WILDFLOWER—DO NOT DISTURB**

SWEET CICELY
Osmorhiza claytoni (Michx.) Clarke
Parsley family   Umbelliferae

woods   late spring   18-36 in. (4.5-9 dm)

Sparse, often scraggly clusters of white to greenish-white inconspicuous flowers. The small blossoms radiate from a central point like a bursting rocket.

Leaves are pinnately compound with each one divided into 3-5 segments; often each segment is again divided into 3 leaflets. Leaf margins are decidedly coarsely toothed. There are often 1 or 2 basal leaves that are similar to the stem leaves. Appearance of leaves may be fernlike, especially in newer, smaller upper leaves. Stems are upright and have some degree of hairiness varying from slight to dense.

CANADA VIOLET
Viola canadensis L.
Violet family   Violaceae

woods   spring-early summer
6-16 in. (1.5-4 dm)

Flowers with 5 white petals, the lower 3 marked at their base with conspicuous, fine, brown-purple veins. Back side of petals is tinged blue or purple. Center of the flower is yellow. Flowers, leaves on the same stem.

Leaves are found both on the stem and at base of plant; basal leaves with very long stalks, roughly 3 times the length of the blades. Stem leafstalks are shorter; blades heart-shaped with sawtooth margins.

Stems are smooth to somewhat downy. One of at least 21 species of violets in the area.

Trillium   B

Nodding Trillium   D

May
Apple

C

Sweet
Cicely

D

Rue
Anemone

C

Canada
Violet

C

DWARF GINSENG
Panax trifolium L.
Ginseng family   Araliaceae

woods, clearings   spring
4-8 in. (10-20 cm)

A rounded cluster of small, white flowers at the tip of the plant; 5 petals and 5 stamens; stamens protrude beyond petals; flowerstalk arises from a whorl of leaves.

Whorl of leaves is near top of stem, usually 3 in number, palmately compound, each with 3-7 stalkless leaflets; margins finely toothed. Fruit is a yellow berry. Toxicity unknown. Not the ginseng of commerce.

SARSAPARILLA
Aralia nudicaulis L.
Ginseng family   Araliaceae

woods   late spring   8-20 in. (2-5 dm)

Commonly 3 (sometimes 4) balls of tiny white to greenish flowers from a single, leafless stalk that appears to come from the ground. Each flower has 5 petals that may be tinged with green or purple. Flowers occur beneath the leaves.

There is only one leaf but appears to be 3. The main leafstalk starts at ground level and terminates in 3 divisions; each subdivision has 5 leaflets that are egg-shaped with long pointed tips and sawtooth margins.

Fruit is a blue-black berry; not edible.

BRISTLY SARSAPARILLA, *Aralia hispida* Vent. (not shown) is related but flower clusters on same stem and above the leaves. Lower stem is very bristly. Plants are taller (up to 3 ft. or 1 m), bloom later (midsummer), usually on sandier, more open sites. Fruit is also a black, inedible berry.

FLOWERING SPURGE
Euphorbia corollata L.
Spurge family   Euphorbiaceae

dry woods, meadows   summer-fall
1-3½ ft. (3-10 dm)

White flowers in open clusters radiating from a whorl of leaves. 5 rounded white bracts resembling petals surround a small cluster of tiny true flowers.

Leaves are long, narrow, stalkless, with smooth margins. Form whorls in upper part of plant, but alternate, single leaves below.

Stems upright and contain milky juice.

CATNIP or Catmint
Nepeta cataria L.
Mint family   Labiatae

meadows   spring-fall   1-4 ft. (3-12 dm)

Individual flowers are tiny, borne in tight clusters at tips of stems. Petals are white with pink or purple spots.

Leaves are arrowhead-shaped with jagged tooth margins, are opposite each other in pairs, 1-3 in. (2.5-8 cm) long, and a lighter color on the underside.

Stems are 4-sided, erect, and covered with fine fuzzy hairs.

PITCHER'S THISTLE
Cirsium pitcheri (Torr.) T. & G.
Composite family   Compositae

dune sand   spring-fall   up to 3 ft. (9 dm)

Flowers are creamy white to pale yellow. Prickle-tipped, modified leaves (bracts) are on the lower part of the flower head.

Leaves are stalkless, deeply cleft into narrow lobes that are either smooth at the tips or end in a small, weak spine.

Stem and lower leaf surfaces are densely white-woolly. Stems are erect and lack spines except where leaves attach to stem.

**A THREATENED SPECIES
DO NOT DISTURB**

LYRE-LEAVED ROCK CRESS
Arabis lyrata L.
Mustard family   Cruciferae

dunes, rocks   spring-fall
up to 14 in. (3.5 dm)

Flowers are about ¼ in. (5 mm) across with 4 rounded, white petals.

Leaves on the stem are few and scattered, long, narrow, and tapered to the base; margins are usually entire but there may be a few slightly toothed leaves on the lower stem. At the base of the plant is a rosette of narrow but deeply lobed leaves.

Stems are upright or somewhat reclining, smooth in upper portion and sometimes fuzzy near the base.

Fruit is a long, narrow pod up to 1½ in. (4 cm) long and only about 1/16 in. (1-2 mm) wide. Pods tend to point upward.

Dwarf Ginseng   D

Catnip

C

Sarsaparilla

D

Pitcher's
Thistle

D

Flowering
Spurge

B

Lyre-leaved
Rock Cress

C

33

BUCKBEAN
Menyanthes trifoliata L.
Gentian family   Gentianaceae

bogs, ponds, swamps
spring-early summer 4-12 in. (1-3 dm)

Flowers are white, sometimes tinged with pink, tubular at the base and flaring to 5 recurved lobes that are conspicuously fringed on the inner surface.

Leaves are palmately compound with 3 shiny leaflets on a long stalk arising from base of the plant. Leaflets are 1-3 in. (2.5-7 cm) long.

Plants are usually found in shallow water.

**PROTECTED MICHIGAN
WILDFLOWER—DO NOT DISTURB**

BEARBERRY or Kinnikinick
Arctostaphylos uva-ursi (L.) Spreng.
Heath family   Ericaceae

dunes, rocky areas spring- early summer
up to 12 in. (3 dm)

Flowers are white, white tinged with pink, or pink. Oval in shape, constricted at the mouth then flaring into 5 spreading lobes. Flowers in clusters of 5-10 at end of branches.

Leaves smooth, leathery, shiny on upper side, persistent year-round, rounded at terminal ends but tapering at the base; margins entire.

Stems mostly prostrate with branches upright, woody with red to gray bark, creeping.

Fruit is a bright red, edible berry. Dry.

CLUSTERED BROOM-RAPE
Orobanche fasciculata Nutt.
Broom-rape family   Orobanchaceae

dune sand spring-summer
2-6 in. (5-15 cm)

Flowers usually white but may be yellow or purple, up to 1 in. (2.5 cm) long, with 5 nearly equal lobes. Calyx is downy, tubular with flaring lobes.

Leaves are white, scalelike.

Stems reddish. Plants parasitic, usually on wormwood in this area. As with parasitic plants chlorophyll is absent, thus no green coloration.

**A THREATENED SPECIES
DO NOT DISTURB**

GREENBRIER
Smilax hispida Muhl.
Lily family   Liliaceae

swales spring-early summer vine

Ragged, open clusters of greenish-white to green flowers, each cluster arising in a leaf axil. Flowerstalk is at least twice as long as the adjacent leafstalk.

Leaves are thin, comparatively large (3-5 in. or 8-12 cm long). Somewhat roundish but with pointed tips. Threadlike tendrils arise from the leaf axils.

Greenish prickles are found along the stem. These turn dark with age. Prickles often few and scattered on upper stem becoming dense to extremely dense on the lower part.

Fruit is clustered dark blue to black, inedible berries.

LESSER STITCHWORT
Stellaria graminea L.
Pink family   Caryophyllaceae

woods, clearings spring-midsummer
12-20 in. (3-5 dm)

The white flowers are borne on spreading flowerstalks. The flowers appear to have 10 petals but actually there are only 5 that are deeply notched to about one half the length of the petal.

Leaves in pairs and opposite, ½-2 in. (1.5-5 cm) long, narrow, margins smooth.

STARWORT   (not shown)
Stellaria longipes   Goldie

Has similar flowers to the Lesser Stitchwort but they are borne on erect stalks and the petals are more deeply cleft. Plants are shorter. Supposedly limited to the Grand Sable Dunes area in Michigan.

PLEASE DO NOT PICK

ENCHANTER'S NIGHTSHADE
Circaea quadrisulcata (Maxim.)
Evening primrose family   Onagraceae

woods summer 1-2 ft. (3-6 dm)

Flowers small, white, sparsely scattered on upright, multiple flowerstalks from a single stem. The 2 petals are so deeply notched as to appear as 4. There are 2 recurved sepals.

Leaves are simple, egg-shaped with pointed tips, opposite on long leafstalks; toothed. Fruit is a small bur covered with hooked bristles.

Buckbean

D

Greenbrier D

Lesser
Stitchwort

D

Bearberry C

Clustered Broom-rape D

Enchanter's Nightshade C

Wild Strawberry
Fragaria virginiana Duchesne.
Rose family   Rosaceae

meadows, open woods
late spring-early summer   3-6 in. (8-15 cm)

White flowers are ½-1 in. (1.2-2.5 cm) across with 5 rounded petals, numerous yellow stamens. Flowers and leaves are on separate stalks, both arising from near the ground line and flowerstalks usually shorter than the leafstalks.

Leaves are compound with 3 blunt-toothed leaflets; leafstalks and underside of leaflets finely hairy.

Fruit is a red berry, fragrant, and bearing seeds in sunken pits on the surface; edible and delicious. The related WOODLAND STRAWBERRY, *Fragaria vesca* L. (not shown) has fruits that bear seeds on the surface, not in pits. The plants are usually smaller, flowers are smaller and borne on stalks usually longer than the leafstalks. Both species are low plants spreading by runners.

Three-Toothed Cinquefoil
Potentilla tridentata Soland.
Rose family   Rosaceae

dry sand, rock crevices   spring-summer
4-12 in. (1-3 dm)

Spreading clusters of 5-petaled white flowers with the flowerstalks rising above a mat of leaves. Numerous stamens are white with pinkish anthers.

Leaves palmately compound with 3 leaflets, each somewhat wedge-shaped. The side margins of the leaflets are entire and hairy but the tip terminates in 3 rounded but sharply pointed teeth. Upper leaf surface is bright green turning brilliant red; lower surface covered with tannish fuzz; leafstalks have long white hairs.

Sticky False Asphodel
Tofieldia glutinosa (Michx.)
Lily family   Liliaceae

wet or moist areas   summer   20 in. (5 dm)

The cluster of white flowers at tip of stem has short flowerstalks. 6 petals and 6 stems with pink anthers. A few long, narrow leaves sheath the stem near base of plant.

Stem (and flowerstalks) covered with short, sticky, black hairs. Fruits are red, globular capsules.

Bladder Campion
Silene cucubalus Wibel.
Pink family   Caryophyllaceae

meadows spring-summer 8-30 in. (2-8 dm)

Open clusters of 5-30 white flowers, each with 5 deeply notched petals arising from a greatly inflated, smooth, 5-lobed, bell-shaped sac (calyx) which is about ½ in. (13 mm) long, has a papery texture, usually pinkish, and often has many netted green or red veins. The threadlike styles project well beyond the petals.

Leaves are in pairs, 1-3 in. (3-8 cm) long, much longer than broad; margins are entire. Leaves are stalkless, often clasping the stem and are smooth.

Stems are usually smooth but may be hairy, and tend to recline on the ground with age rather than remaining erect.

Fleabane
Erigeron strigosus Muhl.
Composite family   Compositae

meadows   spring-fall 2-4 ft. (6-12 dm)

Asterlike flowers, white to pale pink, with 50-100 "petals" (ray flowers) that are more numerous than on asters.

Leaves are narrow, mostly without teeth on the margins but toothed leaves are not infrequent; basal leaves much longer than broad, widest above the center, up to 1 in. (2.5 cm) wide. Stem leaves are much smaller, are long, narrow, and stalkless.

Stems are sparsely leafy, upright, slender, branching and rebranching near the top. Stems and leaves are very hairy, especially on the lower part of the plant.

Black Snakeroot
Sanicula marilandica L.
Parsley family   Umbelliferae

woods spring-early summer 1-4 ft. (3-12 dm)

Flowers are white, sometimes described as greenish-white, yellowish-white, or green. Each blossom is a ball of tiny flowers arising from a whorl of small leaves below.

Basal leaves are palmately compound, each with 5 leaflets, the lower pair so deeply cut as to appear as 7 leaflets; margins are sawtooth to jagged.

Fruit is a bristly bur.

Wild Strawberry   C

Bladder Campion   A

Three-toothed
Cinquefoil

D

Fleabane   A

Sticky
False
Asphodel

C

Black
Snakeroot

D

Dogfennel or Stinking Chamomile
Anthemis cotula L.
Composite family   Compositae

meadows   spring-fall   4-24 in. (1-6 dm)

Daisy-like flowers with 10-20 white "petals" that are ¼-½ in. (6-9 mm) long. Center is a domed, yellow disk. Flower is ¾-1 in. (1.9-2.5 cm) across.

Leaves are deeply cut and finely divided; ill smelling.

Scentless Chamomile (not shown)
Matricaria maritima L.

Flowers similar to *Anthemis cotula* but leaves are even more finely divided, odorless, and blossom later in the season (summer-early fall).

Great Solomon's Seal
Polygonatum canaliculatum (Muhl.) Pursh.
Lily family   Liliaceae

moist woods, thickets, roadsides
early summer   up to 4 ft. (12 dm)

Greenish-white bell-shaped flowers ⅔-¾ in. (15-20 mm) long dangle in clusters of 2 to 10 beneath the arching stem.

Leaves are broadly lance-shaped, 2¼ to 6 in. (5.5-15 cm) long and ¾ to 3 in. (2-8 cm) wide, smooth, stalkless or often clasping the stem. Leaf margins are entire. Stem is stout, smooth, arching.

Fruit is a blue to black many-seeded berry.

Hairy Solomon's Seal (not shown)
P. pubescens (Willd.) Pursh.

Flowers are smaller than *P. canaliculatum* (less than ½ in.) and the leaf veins are minutely hairy on the lower surface.

Prairie or White False Indigo
Baptisia leucantha P. & G.
Bean family   Fabaceae

meadows, woods   summer   3-6 ft. (1-2 m)

Flowers mostly white but may have a tinge of purple; up to 1 in. long (2.5 cm), borne on an erect spike, the flowering portion being up to 2 ft. long. Only one (or a few) flowering spikes per plant.

Leaves palmately compound, the 3 more or less roundish leaflets about 2 in. long (5 cm). Drying leaves tend to turn black.

Fruit is a black 1-2 in. drooping pod.
**A THREATENED SPECIES
DO NOT DISTURB**

False Solomon's Seal
Smilacina racemosa (L.) Desf.
Lily Family   Liliaceae

woods   spring-early summer
16-36 in. (4-9 dm)

Branched clusters of many tiny individual creamy-white flowers borne at tip of stem.

Leaves are large and in a flat plane, a row each side of the stem, oval with pointed tips, 4-8 in. (10-20 cm) long and 1-3 in. (3-8 cm) wide; veins are prominent and parallel; leaf-stalks are very short. Stems are arched (neither standing upright nor reclining on the ground) and covered with fine hairs.

Fruit is a white berry spotted with brown, later turning red dotted with purple. Although the taste is not too bad, the berry does have a very large seed. Not recommended for eating.

Starry False Solomon's Seal
Smilacina stellata (L.) Desf.
Lily family   Liliaceae

A plant similar to *S. racemosa* with these differences:

1. Flowers are fewer but larger, ¼-¾ in. (6-9 mm) across.

2. Leaves are narrower, longer, and lack leaf-stalks so that leaf blade clasps the stem.

3. Fruits are green berries with black stripes or may be completely black. Berries may turn bronze color with age.

4. More likely to be found in the open dunes than in or along wooded areas.

Rock Sandwort
Arenaria stricta Michx.
Pink family   Caryophyllaceae

dunes, rocks   early summer
6-9 in. (15-23 cm)

Flowers white, ½-¾ in. (12-20 mm) across, 5 petals each longer than broad.

Leaves needlelike, paired, often with clusters of smaller ones between the pair, leaves crowded into lower half of stem, upper half essentially without leaves.

Stems are wiry. Plants may form loose, mat-like colonies.

Dogfennel   C

False Solomon's Seal   C

Great Solomon's Seal   D

Starry False
Solomon's
Seal

C

Prairie False
Indigo

C

Rock Sandwort   C

Bastard Toadflax
Comandra umbellata (L.) Nutt.
Sandalwood family   Santalaceae

dry woods, meadows, shores
spring-summer up to 12 in. (3 dm)

Blossoms form a flat-topped cluster of white (may be green tinted), individually small, bell-shaped flowers with flaring tips resembling 5-pointed stars.

Leaves oblong-oval, ¾-1½ in. (2-4 cm) long, numerous and alternate, margins entire; veins obscure.

Northern Comandra (not shown)
Comandra livida Richards.

Smaller than *C. umbellata*, prefers moister sites, and the fruit is a scarlet berry.

Comandras are parasitic with their roots attached to other woody plant roots.

Meadowsweet
Spirea alba DuRoi.
Rose family   Rosaceae

wet meadows, swales summer
up to 7 ft. (2 m)

A tapering spike of separated clusters of tiny flowers about ¼ in. (6 mm) across; petals usually white but may be slightly pink. Numerous projecting stamens give the flower head a fuzzy outline.

Leaves are 1¼-2½ in. (3-6 cm) long.

Margins are finely toothed; leaf surfaces essentially smooth. A woody-stem shrub.

Moth Mullein
Verbascum blattaria L.
Snapdragon family   Scrophulariaceae

meadows summer-fall 1-3 ft. (3-9 dm)

Flowers are white often tinged with purple or commonly, all yellow. Petals 5 in number; stamens have purplish beards and orange anthers. Flowers in a terminal spike attached to plant stem by short flowerstalks that seldom exceed ⅝ in. (15 mm). Flowers 1 in. across (2.5 cm).

Leaves are few and variable in shape and size, larger at bottom of plant; may have entire, toothed, or lobed margins. Leaves are smooth.

Stem upright, slender, fuzzy at top.

Thimbleberry
Rubus parviflorus Nutt.
Rose family   Rosaceae

open woods, meadows early summer
3-6 ft. (1-2 m)

Flowers white, showy, 1-2 in. (3-5 cm) across. Petals oval, 5 in number; stamens yellow and numerous; sepals 5 in number, long pointed. Leaves large, 4-8 in. (10-20 cm) across, usually 5 lobes, margins coarsely and irregularly toothed, the veins are prominent.

Leaves resemble maple leaves in shape.

Fruit is a many seeded, thimble-shaped red berry, edible but tart.

A shrub highly prized for its showy flowers and fruit that is excellent for jam.

White Baneberry or Doll's-Eyes
Actaea alba (L.) Mill.
Crowfoot family   Ranunculaceae

woods early summer 1-3 ft. (3-9 dm)

Elongated, thimble-shaped, dense clusters of white flowers borne on thick flowerstalks; 4-10 petals and numerous stamens; sepals drop as the flower opens.

Leaves 2-3 times pinnately compound; leaflet surfaces smooth; margins sharply and irregularly toothed; lighter color on lower surface.

Fruit is a cluster of rather large, usually white berries, each with a conspicuous dark spot (doll's eyes). Stalks bearing the ripe berries are red. Poisonous to eat.

Red Baneberry
Actaea rubra (Ait.) Willd.
Crowfoot family   Ranunculaceae

woods early summer 1-3 ft. (3-9 dm)

Compared to *A. alba* the white flower cluster is usually more rounded than elongated, the flowerstalks (later becoming the fruit stalks) are finer and more delicate, and the dark spot on the berry is smaller and less conspicuous. Poisonous.

Note: There are white-berried "red" baneberries and red-berried "white" baneberries so fruit color can be misleading in identification.

Bastard Toadflax   C

Thimbleberry   B

Meadowsweet

B

White Baneberry   D

Moth
Mullein

C

Red
Baneberry

D

Purple Meadow-Rue

Thalictrum dasycarpum Fisch. & Avé-Lall.
Crowfoot family   Ranunculaceae

swales, swamps, meadows   summer
3-7 ft. (1-2 m)

Sprays of dangling, white flowers, the most conspicuous parts being the projecting, threadlike stamens. There are no petals and the sepals drop as they unfold. Flowers are usually well above the leaves at the top of the plant.

Leaves are 2-3 times compound, being divided, then divided again, and, finally, into three leaflets. Margins of leaflets may be entire but usually have 3 blunt lobes at their apex. Lower surface of leaflets is distinctly fuzzy.

Stems are thick, many, and usually purplish in color from which the species derives its common name.

Early Meadow-Rue

Thalictrum dioicum L.
Crowfoot family   Ranunculaceae

woods, swales   early spring
12-28 in. (3-7 dm)

The many stamens at maturity are even more decidedly downward pointing than those of *T. dasycarpum*, are yellow to greenish-yellow, and the sepals green to purplish.

Leaves of both species are 2-3 times compound but *T. dioicum* leaflets are often inclined to have more than 3 lobes at the apex. Note: this plant blossoms much earlier in the season, is much smaller, and is more apt to be found in rich wooded areas. Also, it is more common in the southern part of the state than it is in the north.

Partridgeberry

Mitchella repens L.
Madder family   Rubiaceae

dry woods   summer   prostrate

Flowers are in pairs, tubular and flaring into 4 (rarely 3, 5, or 6) white petals that are conspicuously hairy on their inner face. Pink blossoms rarely occur.

Leaves are in pairs, rounded, about ½ in. (12 mm) long, remain green all year.

Stems creeping, forming mats. Roots may be found along the stem.

Fruit is a red berry which persists through the winter. Edible but insipid.

Note: Since the berry rather than the flower is apt to attract attention, this is the illustration used.

Pearly Everlasting

Anaphalis margaritacea (L.) Benth. & Hook.
Composite family   Compositae

meadows   summer   up to 3 ft. (1 m)

Flower heads pearly-white with yellow centers, globular-shaped, densely packed, and borne on short stalks at top of stem.

Leaves densely white-wooly on underside, long-cottony above, alternate on stem, up to 5 in. (12 cm) long, and narrow.

Stems white-wooly. Plant dries well for winter bouquets.

White Snakeroot

Eupatorium rugosum Houtt.
Composite family   Compositae

woods   summer-fall   1-5 ft. (3-15 dm)

Flat-topped clusters of tiny white flowers with 12-24 individual flowers in each cluster.

Leaves in pairs along the stem, egg-shaped with tip drawn out to a sharp point; margins sawtoothed. Leafstalks up to 1 in. (2.5 cm) long or longer on large leaves.

Stems smooth in upper portion, fuzzy to slightly hairy in lower.

Ox-Eye Daisy or Marguerite

Chrysanthemum leucanthemum
Composite family   Compositae

meadows   summer   1-3 ft. (3-9 dm)

Showy flowers with 15-30 white "petals" notched at tips, a yellow center disk depressed in its middle, each flower up to 2 in. (5 cm) across. "Petals" are wider than most asters or fleabanes.

Leaves are smooth or sparsely hairy. Stem leaves are stalkless, base of leaf often clasping the stem; length up to 2 in. (5 cm), narrow, dark green; margins coarsely toothed.

Stems are upright, smooth or sparsely hairy. Plants commonly found in extensive colonies.

Purple
Meadow-rue

B

Pearly
Everlasting

B

Early
Meadow-rue

D

White
Snakeroot

C

Partridgeberry   D

Ox-eye Daisy   A

43

Cow Parsnip
Heracleum lanatum Michx.
Parsley family   Umbelliferae

meadows   summer   up to 10 ft. (3 m)

Flat-topped clusters of white flowers form very large blossoms up to 8 in. (20 cm) across. Petals deeply notched at tip, those on outer edge of cluster larger than those on inside.

Leaves very large, commonly up to 12-18 in. (3-4.5 dm) across, compound with 3 coarsely toothed leaflets, hairy on underside; leafstalks inflated and clasp stem.

Stem definitely ridged, woolly and hollow, up to 2 in. (5 cm) thick.

Plants are conspicuous because of their huge size.

Water-Hemlock
Cicuta maculata L.
Parsley family   Umbelliferae

meadows, swamps, streambanks
summer-fall   3-6 ft. (1-2 m)

Starburst clusters of tiny white flowers at tip of flowerstalks above the leaves. Clusters 2-4 in. (5-10 cm) across.

Leaves are 2 or 3 times pinnately compound (there are secondary leafstalks arising from the main leafstalk). Leaflets are long, narrow, sharp pointed, and have sawtooth margins.

Stem is smooth, coarse, erect, and many branched; often a tendency to have a purple color, especially in lower portion.

All parts of this plant, particularly the roots, are deadly poisonous when eaten.

Wild Carrot or Queen Anne's Lace
Daucus carota L.
Parsley family   Umbelliferae

meadows   summer-fall   2-3 ft. (6-9 dm)

Flower head is a flat-topped cluster of small, creamy-white, individual flowers. There may be one or more dark colored flowers in the center. Immediately below the flower head are several 3-5 pronged, narrow, sharp pointed, modified leaves (bracts).

Leaves are deeply and finely cut. The leafstalk is bristly.

Stems are stiff, erect, and bristly. Plant has a strong carrot odor.

Caution: Handling the leaves may cause a skin rash on some people.

Field Bindweed
Convolvulus arvensis L.
Morning Glory family   Convolvulaceae

dunes, meadows   summer   trailing

Flowers white, pink, or white tinged with pink. Petals are united into a funnel-shaped flower about 1 in. (2-3 cm) across.

Leaves opposite, minutely downy, the arrowhead-shaped blades attached to a short leafstalk.

Stems are prostrate, trailing, or twining on surrounding vegetation.

Hoary Alyssum
Berteroa incana (L.) DC.
Mustard family   Cruciferae

meadows   summer-early fall
1-2 ft. (3-6 dm)

Flowers white, tiny, in elongated clusters at tip of stem; the 4 petals are deeply notched, sepals and flowerstalks are hairy. The stalkless leaves are much longer than broad, wider across the middle and tapering to both ends; margins are smooth.

Leaves and stems are covered with a pale hoary down.

Stems are rigidly upright.

Seed pods are usually present below the flowers, are oval but have pointed tips.

Dune Lily or Death Camas
Zygadenus glaucus Nutt.
Lily family   Liliaceae

dunes, beaches   summer   1-3 ft. (3-9 dm)

6 greenish-white "petals" that may also be bronze or purple on the underside. Each "petal" has a heart-shaped greenish gland at its base. These "petals" are actually 3 true petals and 3 sepals.

Leaves are grasslike, found mostly at the base of the plant, are very long (up to 20 in. or 5 dm) and narrow, decreasing in size higher on the stem; leathery.

Stems are smooth and stiffly erect.

All parts of this plant are poisonous if eaten.

Cow
Parsnip

B

Field Bindweed   C

Water-
hemlock

C

Hoary Alyssum   C

Dune
Lily

D

Wild Carrot   A

GREEN SHINLEAF
Pyrola virens Schweigg.
Heath family   Ericaceae

dry woods   early summer
6-10 in. (1.5-2.5 dm)

Spikes of 2-13 white to greenish, waxy, green veined flowers with protruding styles.

Leaves all at base of plant, long-stalked, leaf blades shorter than leafstalks; blades rounded, tapering to a point.

Stems mostly naked with, perhaps, one scale leaf about halfway up.

SIDEBELLS or One-Sided Shinleaf
Pyrola secunda L.
Heath family   Ericaceae

woods, bogs   summer
4-10 in. (10-25 cm)

Flowers white to greenish arising from one side of flowerstalk.

Stalk often bent allowing blossoms to dangle as little bells.

Style is long and straight and exceeds the length of the petals.

Leaves basal, roundish, blades are longer than leafstalks.

SHINLEAF
Pyrola elliptica Nutt.
Heath family   Ericaceae

woods   summer   5-10 in. (13-26 cm)

White, nodding, waxy blossoms in a loose spike; 5 petals usually with green veins; a long, curving pistil extends beyond the petals. Flowers are fragrant.

Leaves only at bottom of the plant with leaf blades longer than the leafstalks and longer than broad (up to 3 in. or 7 cm long).

Blade "flows" into leafstalk. Color is dull green.

Stem is smooth, leafless in upper portion.

Most common of all the pyrolas.

PLEASE DO NOT PICK

WATER PARSNIP
Sium suave Walt.
Parsley family   Umbelliferae

swamps, meadows, swales   summer
up to 6 ft. (1.8 m)

Blossoms are white, flat-topped clusters of tiny individual flowers at tips of flowerstalks that radiate from the top of the stem or lateral branches.

Leaves alternate along the stem, are pinnately compound with 3-7 pairs of long, narrow leaflets whose margins are sharply toothed. Basal leaves are finely dissected.

Stem is strongly ridged branching mainly above its middle. Plant prefers wet areas.

Water Hemlock (p 44) has a smooth stem.

WOODNYMPH
or One-Flowered Wintergreen
Moneses uniflora (L.) Gray.
Heath family   Ericaceae

bogs, swales, swamps   summer
2-5 in. (5-13 cm)

A single white or pinkish flower nodding from tip of stem, ½-¾ in. (13-20 mm) across, and fragrant. Has a prominent, melon-like, green pistil with a protruding style; 5 waxy petals.

Leaves are at base of plant, small, short-stalked, round, shiny below, dull green above; margins may be smooth or finely toothed.

Note: Leaves seen at base of the plant in illustration are not those of woodnymph.

WINTERGREEN or Checkerberry
Gaultheria procumbens L.
Heath family   Ericaceae

dry woods   summer   3-7 in. (8-18 cm)

Flowers are small, white, waxy, egg-shaped, nodding, single blossoms attached to a red-colored flowerstalk.

Leaves are thick, egg-shaped, shiny green, and occur at the top of the plant; persist year-round.

Stems are creeping, woody, and wiry.

Crushed leaves have the odor and taste of wintergreen.

Fruit is an edible red berry often persisting year-round.

Green
Shinleaf

D

Water
Parsnip

C

Sidebells

D

Woodnymph   D

Shinleaf

C

Wintergreen   D

Indian Pipe

Monotropa uniflora L.
Heath family   Ericaceae

woods, swamps   summer-early fall
5-10 in. (13-26 cm)

A single, nodding tubular flower that is the same color as stem; usually white but may be pinkish; entire plant turns black with age.

Leaves are rudimentary, scalelike, white to pink.

Stem is white to pink, smooth and waxy in appearance. A parasitic plant lacking chlorophyll, thus no green coloration.

PLEASE DO NOT PICK

Poison Ivy or Three-Leaved Ivy

Rhus radicans L.
Cashew family   Anacardiaceae

meadows, woods, dunes   early summer
prostrate or climbing vine

Very inconspicuous 5-petaled, small, white to greenish-white flowers, clustered in leaf axils.

Leaves have 3 leaflets from a common point, mostly oblong with a pointed tip, margins are entire but there may be one or more irregular lobes along the side; color is a shiny green turning to a brilliant red later in the season. Leaf size, shape are highly variable.

Fruit is a cluster of white to grayish-white, shiny berries. The berries are poisonous. In fact, all parts of the plant are poisonous to touch, causing painful, itching blisters of the skin. Contact is to be avoided at any time of the year including the dormant season. Even smoke from burning plants carries the irritant and can cause the same symptoms as touching the plant.

Poison ivy may be erect as individual plants, may climb on fences, trees, or, most commonly, form mats over the surface of the ground.

A person is more apt to be attracted to the lustrous green or red leaves than to the flowers or fruit, which are inconspicuous, so remember the saying:

LEAFLETS THREE, LET IT BE!

Culver's Root

Veronicastrum virginicum (L.) Farw.

Figwort family   Scrophulariaceae

meadows, open woods   summer
2-6 ft. (6-18 dm)

White or pink, tubular flowers in long tapering spikes; 2 stamens extend beyond the petals of each flower.

Long, narrow, pointed leaves in whorls of 3-6 around the stem; margins sawtoothed.

Pale Painted Cup

Castilleja septentrionalis Lindl.
Figwort family   Scrophulariaceae

sandy or gravelly shores, woods
summer   6-24 in. (1.5-6 dm)

What appear to be flowers are white to yellowish leafy bracts with the small, tubular white or yellowish flowers hidden among these. Leaves narrow and 1-4 in. (3-10 cm) long, attached singly and alternately along the stem; margins are smooth.

Stems are upright, ridged, and sometimes streaked.

See Indian Paintbrush, *Castilleja coccinea*.

**A THREATENED SPECIES
DO NOT DISTURB**

Cow Wheat

Melampyrum lineare Desr.
Figwort family   Scrophulariaceae

woods, bogs, rock crevices   summer
4-12 in. (1-3 dm)

Tubular, white flowers with a yellow tip on the lower lip, found in leaf axils (where leaf joins the stem).

Leaves in pairs, long and narrow, margins usually smooth except upper leaves may be toothed near their base.

Stems are purplish and fuzzy.

Turtlehead

Chelone glabra L.
Figwort family   Scrophulariaceae

swales, wet meadows   summer-fall
18-36 in. (4.5-9 dm)

Flowers are tubular, creamy-white, sometimes tinged with pink or purple, formed in tight, upright clusters at tip of the stem.

Leaves are in pairs along the stem, are stalkless, long, narrow, and sawtoothed along the margins.

Indian Pipe

D

Pale
Painted Cup

C

Poison Ivy

D

Cow
Wheat

D

Culver's
Root

B

Turtlehead

B

49

Round-Leaved Sundew
Drosera rotundifolia L.
Sundew family   Droseraceae

bogs, swamps   summer
up to 9 in. (23 cm)

Flowers (not pictured) are white to pink, tiny, 1/16-¼ in. (4-7 mm) across; 3-15 in a loose spike on a tall flowerstalk.

The leaves are the conspicuous part of the plant and are basal, with round, saucer-shaped blades on long, flattened leafstalks, the entire leaf covered with bristly red hairs with a clear, sticky exudate at their tips.

These curious leaves trap and digest insects.

White Water Lily or
Tuberous Water Lily
Nymphaea tuberosa   Paine
Water Lily family   Nymphaeaceae

aquatic   summer   floating

Floating white flowers with concentric rows of tapered petals; outer rings of petals larger than those in center. There is a yellow disk in the center of the blossom.

Leaves are large, flat, round with a deep notch at the base, long-stalked, lower surface green to dull purple.

Flowers not especially fragrant.

White Campion or Evening Lychnis
Lychnis alba Mill.
Pink family   Caryophyllaceae

meadows   summer-early fall
18-48 in. (4.5-12 dm)

Flowers have 5 white, deeply notched petals attached to a more or less inflated sac. The threadlike styles are mostly contained within the flower tube, seldom extending beyond the petals. In contrast to Bladder Campion the sac is definitely hairy, usually more tubular than bell-shaped; the sac (calyx) of a mature flower is greenish and usually has green veins but (rarely) these may be reddish-brown; veins are roughly parallel and extend from the base of the calyx (sac) to its tip. Flowers tend to open in the evening.

Leaves are opposite, hairy, ½-1½ in. (1-4 cm) long; margins entire.

Stems are hollow and coarsely hairy.

Common or Nodding Ladies'- Tresses
Spiranthes cernua (L.) Rich.
Orchid family   Orchidaceae

bog, wet meadows   late summer-fall
8-18 in. (20-46 cm)

A terminal spike of nodding white flowers arranged in a double spiral along the central stem.

Leaves mostly at the base of the plant, long (up to 12 in. or 30 cm), very narrow. Stem leaves are greatly reduced in size, sometimes a mere scalelike projection.

PROTECTED MICHIGAN WILDFLOWER—DO NOT DISTURB

Cut-Leaved Water-Horehound
Lycopus americanus Muhl.
Mint family   Labiatae

swamps, wet areas   summer-fall
6-24 in. (1.5-6 dm)

Flowers are white, tiny, in dense whorled clusters around the stem in leaf axils.

Leaves longer than wide, opposite each other in pairs. Margins of leaves on upper stem are coarsely toothed; tip ends of the lower leaves are similarly coarsely toothed but the portion of the margins closer to the leafstalk are deeply cleft into sharp pointed lobes.

Stems are 4-sided, usually smooth but may be somewhat hairy, especially in the area where the leaves attach to the stem.

Boneset or Thoroughwort
Eupatorium perfoliatum L.
Composite family   Compositae

bogs, swales, meadows   summer-fall
18 in.-5 ft. (4.5-15 dm)

Flat-topped clusters of dull white (rarely purple) flowers with 9-23 blossoms in each flower head. Each individual flower appears to be a tuft of rodlike filaments with no apparent petals.

Leaves in pairs opposite each other, broad at base and surrounding the stem so the stem appears to pierce the leaves; slightly fuzzy on the upper surface and even more definitely hairy on the lower surface.

Stem is conspicuously hairy.

white

Common
Ladies'-
tresses

D

Round-leaved Sundew   D

Cut-leaved
Water-
Horehound

D

White Water Lily   B

Boneset

B

White Campion   C

51

YARROW
Achillea millefolium L.
Composite family   Compositae

meadows   summer-fall   1-3 ft. (3-9 dm)

Flat-topped flower clusters made up of many, small, individual, 5-petaled blossoms. Usually white, sometimes pinkish.

Leaves finely cut into many small divisions; increase in size from top to bottom of plant.

Stems are smooth or covered with white-cottony fuzz. Plant has a strong aroma.

FLAT-TOPPED ASTER
Aster umbellatus Mill.
Composite family   Compositae

swales, streambanks, meadows
late summer   2-7 ft. (6-21 dm)

Flat-topped clusters of white, sometimes purple-tinged, few "petaled" (7-14) flowers; individual flowers ½-¾ in. (12-19 mm) across.

Leaves are variable in size but always long and narrow, up to 6 in. (16 cm) long, tapered at each end. Lower leaves are smaller than upper and soon dry up; stalkless; margins entire but rough to the touch.

WHITE LETTUCE
Prenanthes alba L.
Composite family   Compositae

woods   late summer-fall
18 in.-5 ft. (4.5-15 dm)

Bell-shaped, drooping, fragrant flowers that are white, yellow-white, or pink with purplish bracts at their bases.

Leaves on lower stem are long-stalked, mostly triangular in outline with variations having 3-5 sharp pointed lobes. Leaves on upper stem are smaller, short-stalked, more oblong than triangular.

Stems are smooth, stout, and exude milky juice when cut or broken.

GRASS-OF-PARNASSUS
Parnassia glauca Raf.
Saxifrage family   Saxifragaceae

bogs, swamps, meadows   summer-fall
8-20 in. (2-5 dm)

5-petaled white flowers, ¾-1½ in. (2-4 cm) across with distinct, green veins in the petals. Flowers solitary atop a nearly leafless stem. 5 prominent stamens arise between the petals.

Leaves mostly basal with one small clasping leaf about midway on the stem, margins smooth.

SMALL GRASS-OF-PARNASSUS
P. parviflora   DC.   (not shown)

Smaller than *P. glauca*, the height, leaves, and blossoms being only about half the size. Flowering time commences a little earlier (June).

VIRGIN'S BOWER or Old Man's Beard
Clematis virginiana L.
Crowfoot family   Ranunculaceae

open woods and edges   summer-early fall
vine

White foamy clusters of flowers whose 4 sepals look like petals. There are no true petals, just numerous and conspicuous creamy yellow stamens resembling bristles. Flowers arise from the leaf axils.

Each leaf composed of 3 leaflets on stalks of approximately equal length; stalk of the terminal leaflet is slightly longer than the other two. Margins are coarsely, sharply toothed.

Stems are viny, supported by surrounding vegetation.

Fruits are clusters of seeds, each seed terminated with long, 1-2 in. (2.5-5 cm) silky plumes. From this feature comes the name, Old Man's Beard.

WILD CUCUMBER or Balsam-Apple
Echinocystis lobata (Michx.) T.&G.
Gourd family   Cucurbitaceae

woods, streambanks   summer-early fall
vine

6-petaled white to greenish-white flowers. Male flowers on elongated, erect stalks from leaf axils; female flowers are also from leaf axils but are fewer, less conspicuous, and on shorter stalks.

Leaves resemble maple leaves with 3-7 but usually 5 sharp-pointed, triangular lobes. Leafstalks are about as long as the leaf blade.

Stem is a 4-sided vine climbing on adjacent supports or vegetation by means of stringlike forked tendrils.

Fruit is an inflated, greenish bladder, 1-2 in. (2.5-5 cm) long, covered with weak bristles.

Yarrow

A

Grass-of-Parnassus   C

Flat-topped
Aster

C

Virgin's Bower   B

White Lettuce

C

Wild Cucumber   C

Marsh Marigold or Cowslip
Caltha palustris L.
Crowfoot family   Ranunculaceae

swamps, swales, streams   spring
1-2 ft. (3-6 dm)

Conspicuous yellow flowers ½-1½ in. (12-38 mm) across with 5-9 "petals."

Leaves are smooth, shiny, rounded or heart-shaped, as large as a person's hand; indented at base; margins are sawtoothed.

Stems are stout, erect, and hollow.

A plant of wet places, even into shallow water. More likely to be found growing in colonies blanketing somewhat extensive areas rather than as individual plants.

Buttercup
Ranunculus acris L.
Crowfoot family   Ranunculaceae

wet meadows, swales   spring-fall
2-3 ft. (6-9 dm)

Flowers are yellow with 5-7 glossy, overlapping petals. The bushy stamens are prominent in the center of the flower.

Leaves on the lower stem are divided into 3 segments, each deeply and sharply lobed. Upper leaves are greatly reduced in size and complexity. Leaves are hairy, especially on the lower surface.

Stems are smooth at the upper end but usually very hairy on the lower portion.

Yellow Trout Lily or Adder's Tongue
Erythronium americanum Ker.
Lily Family   Liliaceae

woods   spring   6-10 in. (15-26 cm)

Flowers yellow, nodding, one per plant; 6 backward curving petals. Back side of petals often purple or brownish-purple. 6 prominent red-brown or yellow anthers extend beyond the bell-shaped blossom.

Leaves 2, at base of plant, often conspicuously mottled with brown. Plants usually found in colonies with many sterile (nonblossoming) plants.

Fawn Lily (not shown)
E. albidum Nutt.

This species is closely related to Yellow Trout Lily but the flower is white and the leaves are not mottled. Very rare.

PLEASE DO NOT PICK EITHER OF THESE

Large-Flowered Bellwort
Uvularia grandiflora Sm.
Lily family   Liliaceae

woods   spring   8-20 in. (2-5 dm)

6-petaled, bell-shaped, tubular, yellow flowers up to 2 in. (5 cm) long. Blossoms (and leaves) tend to droop as though the plant were wilting.

Leaves are broad and up to 5 in. (13 cm) long, smooth on the upper surface and faintly fuzzy on the lower; veins parallel.

Base of leaf clasps the stem to appear as though the stem passes through the leaf.

Indian Cucumber-Root
Medeola virginiana L.
Lily family   Liliaceae

woods   late spring   1-3 ft. (3-9 dm)

Greenish-yellow flowers from tip of plant on long, slender stalks that permit the flowers to dangle beneath the upper whorl of leaves. Petals curve backward. 3 spreading, brownish colored, threadlike styles from top of ovary.

Leaves are in whorls, one whorl of 5-9 midway up stem, a second whorl of 3-5 at top of stem. Leaves are wide but taper to each end.

Fruit is a dark purple berry. Toxicity unknown. **Caution!**

Clintonia or Bluebead Lily
Clintonia borealis (Ait.) Raf.
Lily family   Liliaceae
woods, cedar swamps
spring, early summer   6-15 in. (15-38 cm)

Bell-shaped, mostly nodding, yellow to greenish-yellow flowers on a leafless stalk; anthers extend well beyond the petals.

Leaves are thick, broad, essentially oblong, up to 12 in. (3 dm) long and 4 in. (1 dm) wide. Usually 2 or 3 leaves at base of plant but there may be 4; margins are finely hairy; veins are parallel to the midrib. Base of leafstalk sheaths the stem.

Fruit is a blue berry (Aug-Sept). Toxic.

PLEASE DO NOT PICK

Marsh Marigold   B

Large-flowered Bellwort   C

Buttercup

B

Indian Cucumber-root   D

Yellow
Trout Lily

C

Clintonia   C

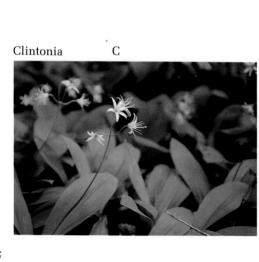

55

Tufted Loosestrife
Lysimachia thyrsiflora L.
Primrose family   Primulaceae

swales, wet meadows
spring-midsummer   1-2 ft. (3-6 dm)

Tufts or balls of yellow flowers on short flowerstalks from leaf axils near middle of stem. Numerous projecting stamens that are nearly twice as long as the petals.

Leaves are long, 2-4 in. (5-10 cm), narrow, opposite in pairs.

Stems are erect and hairy.

Downy Yellow Violet
Viola pubescens Ait.
Violet family   Violaceae

woods   spring and fall   4-12 in. (1-3 dm)

Yellow, pansylike flowers at top of stem. Petals have brown-purple lines at their base, the two side petals bearded.

Leaves are on the same stem with flowers, heart-shaped, usually 2-4 on a stem, and there may be 1-2 basal leaves. Leafstalks, veins, and leaf margins are downy.

Stems are also downy, 1 or 2 per plant.

Essentially a spring flowering plant but may rebloom in the fall.

Smooth Yellow Violet (not shown)
V. eriocarpa Schw.

Has more basal leaves (1-5) than *V. pubescens*. Stems and leaves are smooth or only very sparsely downy.

Coreopsis or Tickseed
Coreopsis lanceolata L.
Composite family   Compositae

dunes, dry woods, meadows
spring-summer   2-3 ft. (6-9 dm)

Flowers are conspicuously bright yellow, borne singly at tips of long stems. There are 8 "petals" each having 3-7 but usually 4 lobes at its tip. There are 2 sets of bracts at the base of flower.

Leaves are long and narrow and found mainly on the lower part of the plant.

Stems are smooth, tend to stand erect but may be found in a reclining position.

Golden Ragwort
Senecio aureus L.
Composite family   Compositae

swamps, swales   spring-early summer
1-3 ft. (3-9 dm)

Flowers are on slender stalks forming flat-topped heads. Each of the several flowers is bright yellow, ½-1 in. (12-25 mm) in diameter, with 8-12 "petals" (ray flowers) surrounding a mass of yellow disk flowers. Bracts below the blossom are often purple tipped.

Plant has both basal and stem leaves present. Basal leaves are heart-shaped with blunt tips; leafstalks are long; leaves often reddish on lower surface. Stem leaves are much narrower, deeply cleft into lobes, alternate on the stem, and are stalkless.

Common Dandelion
Taraxacum officinale Weber
Composite family   Compositae

meadows, lawns   spring-fall
2-18 in. (5-46 cm)

Flower is borne at the tip of the erect flowerstalk that arises from ground level, is leafless, hollow, exudes a milky juice when cut or broken. The solitary yellow flower head is up to 2 in. (5 cm) wide, composed of many tiny individual florets. Calyx is recurved (turns downward away from petals).

Leaves form a basal rosette, are deeply cleft forming pointed lobes facing downward (toward the base of the leaf).

Seeds are borne in a conspicuous, round, fuzzy ball.

Goat's Rue or Rabbit Pea
Tephrosia virginiana (L.) Pers.
Bean family   Fabaceae

dry meadows, woods   early summer
8-20 in. (2-5 dm)

Bicolored red and yellow flowers in clusters at end of main stem or lateral branches.

Leaves pinnately compound; leaflets oval, 8-14 pairs and one terminal leaflet.

Fruit is a very hairy pod 1½-2 in. long (3.5-5.5 cm). Plant is conspicuously covered with soft, light-colored hairs.

56

Tufted Loosestrife   D

Golden Ragwort   B

Downy Yellow Violet   C

Common
Dandelion

A

Coreopsis   A

Goats Rue   C

57

WOOD BETONY or Lousewort
Pedicularis canadensis L.
Figwort family   Scrophulariaceae

dry woods   late spring
6-16 in. (1.5-4 dm)

Loose clusters of tubular flowers at tips of stems; color often yellow but may be red or combinations of yellow and red. Tubular blossoms flare into 2 lips; the upper one is hood-like and longer than the lower.

Leaves are long, narrow, with deeply notched margins. Most of the leaves are at the base of the plant, but there are some stem leaves and these decrease in size from bottom to top of plant.

Leaves are very hairy and are often red.

YELLOW LADY'S-SLIPPER
Cypripedium calceolus L.
Orchid family   Orchidaceae

swamps, bogs, wet woods   late spring
1-2 ft. (3-6 dm)

Flower is a yellow, inflated pouch, single or sometimes 2 per stem. Petals are long, narrow, twisted, and mottled with brown or purple.

Stem is leafy with 3-6 broad, parallel veined leaves that somewhat sheath the stem.

**PROTECTED MICHIGAN
WILDFLOWER—DO NOT DISTURB**

YELLOW WOOD-SORREL
Oxalis stricta L.
Wood-sorrel family   Oxalidaceae

meadows   late spring-fall
prostrate to 18 in. (46 cm)

Yellow, 5-petaled flowers are ¼-½ in. (6-13 mm) across; base of petals may be reddish. Flowerstalks are much longer than leafstalks.

Leaves are clover-like with 3 dark green leaflets radiating from a central point, each with a distinct notch at its tip.

Leaves, leafstalks, and stems may be quite smooth to very hairy. This plant is often found as a weed in lawns and gardens.

SQUAWROOT
Conopholis americana (L.)   Wallr.
Broomrape family   Orobanchaceae

dry woods   late spring   3-8 in. (8-20 cm)

Tubular, yellow, stalkless flowers emerging from under compact scales, the flowers and scales together forming a cylindrical spike. Lower scales are overlapping, fleshy, pointed, and yellow to yellow-brown in color.

Plant resembles a yellow pine cone standing on end.

Plants usually found in groups. A parasite on tree roots, especially oak.

FALSE HEATHER
Hudsonia tomentosa Nutt.
Rockrose family   Cistaceae

dunes   late spring-early summer
prostrate to 8 in. (20 cm)

Very numerous, 5-petaled yellow flowers, tiny (up to ⅜ in. or 10 mm wide), mostly at the ends of the branches. Stamens are projecting yellow rods with knobbed tips.

Leaves are tiny, scalelike, overlapping, covered with gray-white hairs.

Stems are prostrate to slightly ascending, giving rise to a compact plant form that may be up to 2 ft. (6 dm) across.

HAIRY PUCCOON
Lithospermum caroliniense (Walt.) MacMill.
Borage family   Boraginaceae

dunes, meadows, dry woods
late spring-summer   1-2 feet. (3-6 dm)

Tubular flowers flaring into 5 bright orange-yellow rounded petals. Flowers up to 1 in. (2.5 cm) across.

Leaves are many, 1-2 in. (3-6 cm) long, much longer than broad, hairy; leaf margins entire but hairy. The numerous leaves are alternate along the stem.

Stems arise from a woody base and become many branched as the season advances.

PLEASE DO NOT PICK

HOARY PUCCOON (not shown)
L. canescens (Michx.) Lehm.

A related species also found in the area, is similar but smaller than *L. caroliniense*.

Wood Betony   C

Squawroot   D

Yellow
Lady's-slipper

C

False Heather   C

Hairy
Puccoon

C

Yellow Wood-sorrel   C

59

WILD PARSNIP

Pastinaca sativa L.
Parsley family   Umbelliferae

meadows   spring-fall
2-5 ft. (0.6-1.5 m)

Flower head is flat-topped, made up of open, spreading clusters of individual flowers that are small, yellow, and have 15-25 primary rays ("petals"). Each flower cluster is 2-6 in. (5-15 cm) wide.

Leaves are alternate, pinnately compound with 5-15 leaflets that are so deeply cleft as to appear as many times this number. Leaflets up to 4 in. (10 cm) long, margins sharply toothed and lobed.

Leafstalks clasp the main stem. Both basal and stem leaves present.

Stem is grooved, hairy, erect, and stout.

GOLDEN ALEXANDERS

Zizia aureal (L.) Koch
Parsley family   Umbelliferae

moist meadows   spring   up to 3 ft. (9 dm)

Compared to *Pastinaca sativa* this plant is usually shorter, rarely exceeding 3 ft. (9 dm) in height. The yellow flowers have fewer primary rays (10-18); the lower leaves may be subdivided into 2 or 3 secondary leafstalks and 3 leaflets on each stalk.

It is found in wetter habitats and the flowering period seldom lasts beyond early summer (July).

Stems may be reddish and the crushed stems and leaves have a strong parsley odor.

YELLOW PIMPERNEL

Taenidia integerrima (L.) Drude
Parsley family   Umbelliferae

dry woods, meadows   early summer
1-3 ft. (3-9 dm)

Similar to the two previous species but has oval-shaped leaflets that have entire margins. Stems are smooth. Found in drier habitats.

SMOOTHISH HAWKWEED

Hieracium floribundum Wimm. & Grab.
Composite family   Compositae

meadows   summer   9-32 in. (2-8 dm)

Flowerhead is a semi-open to compact cluster of yellow flowers, each about ¾ in. (2 cm) across; "petals" notched at tips; flower bracts with black spines.

Leaves are 1-6 in. (2.5-14 cm) long, narrow (less than 1 in. or 20 mm), and form a basal rosette. There may be 1 or 2 very small stem leaves. Leaves are mostly smooth on the upper surface with only a few hairs near the margin. On the lower surface there are bristles along the midrib; margins are bristly.

Stems are sparsely covered with bristles and, along with the leaves, may have a thin white coating.

Roots send out many spreading runners to form new plants (rhizomes).

KING DEVIL

Hieracium florentinum All.
Composite family   Compositae

Similar to *H. floribundum* but the leaves are essentially smooth, there are only a few black hairs on the flower bracts, and runners are not present.

YELLOW HAWKWEED or Field Hawkweed (not shown)

Hieracium pratense Tausch.

meadows, dry woods   late spring-summer
1-3 ft. (3-9 dm)

Flowers are in a more compact cluster than *H. floribundum*. Flower bracts and stems are heavily covered with black, spiny hairs. The basal leaves are hairy on both surfaces. Flowering begins a little earlier in the season. This is a yellow version of Orange Hawkweed, *H. aurantiacum*.

YELLOW ROCKET or Winter Cress

Barbarea vulgaris R. Br.
Mustard family   Cruciferae

meadows   spring-summer
1-2 ft. (3-6 dm)

4-petaled, elongated clusters of yellow flowers at tips of flowering branches.

Lower leaves are deeply cleft into one large, rounded, terminal lobe and several small, rounded lobes. Upper leaves are coarsely toothed; bases clasp the stem.

Fruits are long, narrow seedpods.

60

Wild
Parsnip

A

Smoothish
Hawkweed

A

Golden
Alexanders

C

King
Devil

C

Yellow
Pimpernel

C

Yellow
Rocket

A

LEAFY SPURGE
Euphorbia esula L.
Spurge family   Euphorbiaceae

dunes, meadows   spring-fall
1-2 ft. (3-6 dm)

Flowers are small, greenish-yellow, inconspicuous in themselves but surmounting a pair of prominent yellow bracts that might be mistaken for flowers. Bracts rounded with pointed tips.

Leaves are long, ¾-3 in. (2-8 cm), narrow, few and scattered on lower stem, numerous on upper stem; margins entire.

Stems are erect, smooth, and branched.

GOAT'S-BEARD
Tragopogon dubius Scop.
Composite family   Compositae

meadows   summer-fall   1-3 ft. (3-9 dm)

A solitary, yellow flower head at tip of stem, outer "petals" 5-notched at tip and exceeded in length by the long, thin, pointed bracts. The flowerstalk below the blossom is inflated and hollow.

Leaves alternate, grasslike, and clasp stem.

Stems are smooth, upright, and exude a milky juice when cut or broken. Seed head a large, round, feathery ball.

Hybridizes freely so there are variations. *T. pratensis* L. has bracts that are shorter than the "petals" and the flowerstalk is not inflated. Purple Goatsbeard, or Oyster Plant, *T. porrifolius*, is similar to *dubius* but has purple flowers and prefers moister sites.

BUTTERFLY WEED or Orange Milkweed
Asclepias tuberosa L.
Milkweed family   Asclepiacaceae

dunes, meadows   early summer-fall
1-2 ft. (3-6 dm)

Flower clusters are mostly at the top of the stem, occasionally smaller clusters may be found in leaf axils. Color mostly bright orange. Lower part of the flower (calyx) turns backward (reflexed), typical of milkweeds.

Leaves are narrow, 2-4 in. (5-10 cm) long, covered with soft, short hairs. The margins are entire.

Stems are finely hairy. Unlike other milkweeds, this one does not have milky juice.

Seed pods are slender and smooth.

PLEASE DO NOT PICK

WOOD LILY
Lilium philadelphicum L.
Lily family   Liliaceae

dunes, meadows   early summer
1-3 ft. (3-9 dm)

Flowers are cuplike and upward facing, usually reddish-orange but ranging from yellow (rare) to brilliant red. 6 petals with purplish spots at their base.

Stamens project well beyond the petals. There may be one to several flowers in bloom on the same stem at one time.

Leaves mostly in whorls or circles around the stem with 4-8 in a group (there may be a few single leaves scattered along the stem between the whorls); leaves are long, narrow, sharp pointed.

Stem stiffly upright, bears flowers at its tip; covered with a white, powdery substance.

PLEASE DO NOT PICK

MICHIGAN LILY
Lilium superbum L.
Lily family   Liliaceae

moist meadows   summer   3-6 ft. (9-18 dm)

One to many nodding, orange to red-orange, showy flowers up to 3 in. (8 cm) across, all at top of plant, each on its own flowerstalk that may be up to 1 ft. (3 dm) long. 3 petals and 3 petallike sepals are strongly backcurved so their points almost touch behind the flower. 6 extended stamens are very conspicuous.

Leaves mostly in a series of whorls up the stem; long, narrow, pointed at each end.

Stems are rigidly upright and smooth.

DAY LILY
Hemerocallis fulva L.
Lily family   Liliaceae

meadows   early summer   3-6 ft. (9-18 dm)

The upward facing, 6-petaled blossom at the tip of the stem is similar to *Lilium philadelphicum*. However, the flower color is more yellowish-orange, the petals are not spotted but do have prominent darker colored streaks (veins) and turn to a yellow color at their base. Rarely is there more than one blossom open at one time and this lasts for just a day. Flowerstalk is leafless.

Leaves are basal, ½-¾ths the length of the flowerstalk and usually less than 1½ in. (4 cm) wide.

Leafy Spurge

B

Wood Lily   B

Goat's-beard   B

Michigan Lily

B

Butterfly Weed   B

Day Lily

B

63

Black-Eyed Susan or Coneflower
Rudbeckia hirta L.
Composite family   Compositae

meadows summer-fall 1-3 ft. (3-9 dm)

Large, conspicuous flowers with yellow to yellow-orange "petals" that are often darker color near their base. Central disk is brown, sometimes purplish, rarely yellow, and is domed.

Leaves are much longer than broad, very hairy.

Stems are very hairy, erect, and stout.

Orange Hawkweed or
Devil's Paintbrush
Hieracium aurantiacum L.
Composite family   Compositae

meadows summer 8-24 in. (2-6 dm)

Orange to reddish-orange flowers about ⅜-¾ in. (1-2 cm) across in a crowded cluster at the top of the single stem.

Leaves are at the base of the plant and there may be 1 or 2 greatly reduced leaves on the stem; both surfaces of leaves are very hairy.

Stem is very hairy and contains a milky juice, particularly at the base.

Plants usually occur in extensive colonies and may cover entire fields and meadows.

Spotted Jewelweed or Touch-Me-Not
Impatiens biflora Walt.
Touch-Me-Not family   Balsaminaceae

swales, wet meadows
summer-early fall 2-5 ft. (6-15 dm)

Dangling, single, orange blossoms with flaring red to brownish spotted petals and a prominent spur at rear that curves back under the flower. Flowers are about 1 in. (2.5 cm) long.

Leaves smooth, thin, long-stalked, egg-shaped with rounded teeth on the margins.

Stems smooth, succulent, freely branched, exuding watery juice when broken. Swollen at lower leaf joints.

Mature seed pods burst suddenly when touched.

Moneywort
Lysimachia nummularia L.
Primrose family   Primulaceae

swales, wet meadows summer
prostrate

Single yellow flowers on long flowerstalks from leaf axils, 1 in. (2-3 cm) across; 5 petals dotted with dark red.

Leaves in pairs along the creeping stem, are rounded in shape, and have entire margins.

Silverweed
Potentilla anserina L.
Rose family   Rosaceae

moist meadows summer prostrate

Usually 5-petaled (sometimes 6 or more) yellow flowers up to 1 in. (2.5 cm) across on leafless stalks. Each petal and the entire flower is essentially round.

Leaves are pinnately compound with 7 to many leaflets that are somewhat hairy on the upper surface, with prominent, long, silvery hairs beneath (from which the plant derives its name); margins coarsely and sharply toothed. Leaflets are larger at the terminal end of the leaf and are interspersed with much smaller leaflets.

Plants spread by runners that are usually red, long, and hairy.

Sulfur Cinquefoil or
Rough-Fruited Cinquefoil
Potentilla recta L.
Rose family   Rosaceae

meadows summer 1-2 ft. (3-6 dm)

Pale, delicate, yellow flowers with 5 petals, each with a rounded notch at its outer margin. Center of flower is a darker yellow disk.

Leaves at the base and on the lower stem are long-stalked, terminating in 5-7 long, narrow, toothed leaflets that are hairy on both surfaces. Higher on the stem the leaflets are short-stalked or stalkless, much smaller, and may be only 3 in number.

Stems are stout, hairy, and erect.

Black-eyed
Susan

A

Moneywort   D

Orange Hawkweed   A

Silverweed   C

Spotted Jewelweed   C

Sulfur Cinquefoil   B

Smooth Sowthistle
Sonchus uliginosus Bieb.
Composite family   Compositae

meadows summer-fall up to 4 ft. (1.2 m)

Yellow, dandelionlike flowers at ends of upper stems; 1¼-2 in. (3-5 cm) across; "petals" many and narrow, blunt ended with multiple notched tips. Flowerstalks and sepals are smooth.

Leaves alternate, mostly on lower half of stem; larger lower leaves with 2-5 (occasionally 7) lobes each side of midrib. Upper leaves mostly unlobed. Base of leaf clasps stem with rounded, prickly, ear-like projections. Leaf margins soft-spiny.

Stems stout, erect, hollow, and contain milky juice.

Evening Primrose
Oenothera biennis L.
Evening Primrose family   Onagraceae

dunes, dry woods, meadows
summer-fall 2-5 ft. (6-15 dm)

Flowers have 4 broad, yellow petals. There is a cross-shaped structure (stigma) in the center of the flower. Blossoms tend to open late in the day and wilt the next day. The 4 long-pointed, swept-back sepals often appear as only 2.

Leaves are stalkless, 4-8 in. (10-20 cm) long, narrow, smooth to very slightly hairy; leaf margins vary from smooth to a few widely spaced very small teeth.

Stems are stout, upright, reddish in the lower portion, downy to slightly bristly.

Fruit is a long, narrow capsule with the cross-shaped stigma often attached to its tip.

Agrimony
Agrimonia gryposepala Walr.
Rose family   Rosaceae

woods and edges summer
up to 5 ft. (15 dm)

Small, 5-petaled, yellow, wedge-shaped flowers borne on a narrow, often curved spike. Short flowerstalks flare into a bell-shaped calyx tube beneath the petals.

Leaves are pinnately compound with 5-9 comparatively large, equal size leaflets with tiny, variable shaped leaflets interspersed.

Margins of larger leaflets coarsely and bluntly toothed. Conspicuous stipules (leaflike appendages) are found at the base of the leafstalk and surround the hairy stem.

Fruit is a conical-shaped bur with hooked bristles on its upper (flattened) end; sticks to clothing.

Yellow Pondlily or Bullhead Lily
Nuphar variegatum Engelm.
Water Lily family   Nymphaeacea

ponds, still water summer aquatic

Cuplike yellow flowers just above surface of ponds and quiet, shallow water; a large, yellow disk (stigma) in center.

Large, round floating leaves have a narrow notch at the base of the blade; leafstalks are submerged, smooth, flexible, and flattened on the upper side.

Swamp Candle or Yellow Loosestrife
Lysimachia terrestris (L.) BSP.
Primrose family   Primulaceae

wet meadows, wet woods summer
12-30 in. (3-7.5 dm)

Single spike of open to rather densely clustered 5-petaled, yellow flowers at top of plant. Base of petals marked with dark (usually reddish) spots or broken lines.

Leaves are paired and opposite, long and narrow, margins entire. Mature plants often have reddish bulblets in leaf axils.

Stem is smooth, upright, and although it may be branched, usually has a single flowering spike.

Common St. John's-Wort
Hypericum perforatum L.
St. John's-Wort family   Hypericacea

meadows summer-early fall
12-30 in. (3-7.5 dm)

Flowers are yellow, numerous, about 1 in. (2.5 cm) across, 5 petals, and many prominent busy stamens from the center. Many black dots occur along the margins of the petals (a hand lens is useful to see these).

Leaves are in pairs and opposite each other, stalkless and toothless. Tiny translucent dots on leaves may be seen by holding a leaf up to the light.

Stems are smoothed and many branched.

Smooth Sowthistle

B

Yellow Pondlily   B

Swamp
Candle

B

Evening Primrose   B

Agrimony

C

Common St. John's-wort   A

67

GROUND CHERRY
Physalis heterophylla Nees.
Nightshade family   Solanaceae

meadows   summer-early fall
1-3 ft. (3-9 dm)

Bell-shaped flowers borne singly from the leaf axils. Petals are light yellow and become a darker color at their base. Calyx and flowerstalks are very hairy.

Leaves are 1-3 in. (2-8 cm) long, pointed at the tips, broadly rounded at the base; margins are smooth or slightly wavy. Leafstalks and upper and lower leaf surfaces are fuzzy. Leaves often have ragged holes caused by insect feeding.

Stems are very hairy and may be sticky.

Fruit is a berry enclosed in the inflated, yellow-green sac. Flowers and fruits commonly on the plant at the same time.

Ripe berries are supposedly edible but are rather tasteless and seedy. Unripe berries are poisonous, use caution.

BUTTER-AND-EGGS
Linaria vulgaris Hill.
Figwort family   Scrophulariaceae

meadows   summer-fall 12-32 in. (3-8 dm)

Many flowers on an upright spike; yellow with an orange marking near the center of the blossom; there is a thick, long-pointed spur at the base. Each flower is about 1 in. (2.5 cm) long including the spur.

Leaves are very numerous, pale green, long, narrow, and pointed at both ends.

Plants spread by underground runners forming colonies of individual plants.

COMMON MULLEIN or Aaron's Rod
Verbascum thapsus L.
Figwort family   Scrophulariaceae

meadows   summer-early fall
3-6 ft. (9-18 dm)

A long, upright spike at the tip of the stem bears the flower buds and scattered, open, yellow flowers with 5 rounded petals.

Although only a few flowers appear at one time, the flowering period extends through the entire summer to fall season.

Leaves are thick and woolly, largest at the base of the plant and getting progressively smaller higher on the stem.

Stem is tall, erect, stout, and densely woolly.

BIRDSFOOT TREFOIL
Lotus corniculatus L.
Bean family   Fabaceae

meadows   summer-fall
prostrate to 2 ft. (6 dm)

Yellow, pea-shaped flowers in clusters of 3-6 at ends of stems.

Compound leaves with 5 leaflets, 3 in cloverlike fashion at the end of the leafstalk and 2 more at its base.

Fruits are long, narrow capsules (pods) radiating from a central point, giving the appearance of a many-toed bird's foot.

A crop found in farm fields, it has escaped to roadsides and other non-cultivated areas. Most prevalent in the eastern Upper Peninsula.

PINESAP
Monotropa hypopithys L.
Heath family   Ericaceae

woods   summer-fall   4-12 in (1-3 dm)

A cluster of 3-10 nodding, pale yellow, tan, or reddish (but never white) flowers from tip of a single stem.

Leaves are scalelike, pressed close to stem, and are the same color as the flowers.

Stem is fleshy and soft.

A saprophytic plant deriving its food from woodland humus. Usually associated with oak trees and sometimes with pine trees.

HORSEMINT
Monarda punctata L.
Mint family   Labiatae

dunes, meadows   summer-fall
1-3 ft. (3-9 dm)

A ring (whorl) of yellow, 2-lipped flowers spotted with purple emerging from a tubed, green calyx above another ring of whitish or purplish bracts (modified leaves). There is usually more than one ring of flowers per stem. The upper lip of each flower is strongly arched.

Leaves are ¾-3 in. (2-8 cm) long, narrow, somewhat fuzzy, occur in pairs with another pair of much smaller leaves at their base.

Stems are erect, square in cross section (4-sided), covered with fine fuzz.

Ground Cherry   C

Birdsfoot Trefoil   A

Butter-and-eggs

A

Pinesap

D

Common
Mullein

B

Horsemint   D

69

Woodland Sunflower
Helianthus divaricatus L.
Composite family   Compositae

wood edges, meadows   summer-early fall
2-5 ft. (6-15 dm)

Flowers are large, 1½-3 in. (4-8 cm) across, showy yellow, with 8-15 long, narrow "petals." Blossoms may be solitary or few per stem but occasionally are numerous. Center of flower is yellow.

Leaves are mostly paired and opposite; either stalkless or with very short stalks; rough on the upper surface and hairy on the lower; length is 2-6 in. (5-15 cm) and up to 3 in. (8 cm) wide.

Stems are smooth and often covered with a grayish, waxy coating.

Tall or Green-Headed Coneflower
Rudbeckia laciniata L.
Composite family   Compositae

swamps, moist meadows   summer-fall
3-10 ft. (1-3 m)

Flowers 2½-4 in. (6-16 cm) wide with 6-10 recurved (drooping) "petals" (rayflowers). Center of flower is a globe-shaped greenish-yellow knob that usually elongates as the flower matures. There is a single flower on each flowerstalk.

Leaves are single, entire to 3-lobed in upper part of plant; lower leaves are pinnately compound with 5-7 irregularly toothed leaflets.

Stems are woody at the base, smooth.

Tall Sunflower
Helianthus giganteus L.
Composite family   Compositae

swamps, moist meadows
late summer-fall   4-10 ft. (1.2-3 m)

Flowers 2-3 in. (5-7.5 cm) across, sometimes single but usually several; 10-20 yellow "petals" (rayflowers). Central disk flowers are yellow to brownish. Flower bracts are long and pointed.

Leaves are simple, have pointed tips, are alternate along the upper stem but may be opposite on the lower stem. Upper leaf surface is rough and the lower surface is finely hairy. Margins are entire to shallow-toothed.

Stems are rough and hairy and often reddish.

Canada Goldenrod
Solidago canadensis L.
Composite family   Compositae

meadows   summer-fall   1-5 ft. (3-15 dm)

Feathery plumes of tiny yellow flowers at tip of stem.

There are many leaves that are long, narrow, smooth, with coarsely sawtoothed margins. Midrib and veins on lower leaf surface may be hairy.

Stem is smooth near the bottom, noticeably downy in upper part.

Bluestem Goldenrod
Solidago caesia L.
Composite family   Compositae

woods and edges   late summer-fall
1-3 ft. (3-9 dm)

Tufts of tiny yellow flowers attached to the main stem at points where leaves are also attached (leaf axils).

Leaves are long, narrow, stalkless, taper to a pointed tip; surfaces are usually smooth but may have a few short hairs along the veins; margins are entire to sawtoothed.

Stems are smooth, usually with a blue or purple coating that can be rubbed off.

Common Tansy
Tanacetum vulgare L.
Composite family   Compositae

meadows   summer-fall   1-4 ft. (3-12 dm)

A flat-topped cluster of many bright yellow flower heads, ¼-¾ in. (5-10 mm) across; formed only at tip of stem. Flowers appear to have no petals resemble yellow buttons.

Leaves are alternate, deeply cut (almost to the midrib) lobes with sawtooth margins, surfaces smooth or nearly so.

Stems mostly smooth and ridged. An aromatic but poisonous plant if ingested.

Huron Tansy   (not shown)
T. huronense Nutt.

Similar to *T. vulgare* but flowers are fewer, larger, and may have very short, inconspicuous "petals;" leaves and stems are hairy.

Habitat is more closely related to the beaches along the northern Great Lakes.

**A THREATENED SPECIES
DO NOT DISTURB**

Woodland
Sunflower

B

Canada
Goldenrod

B

Tall Coneflower B

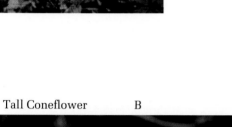

Bluestem
Goldenrod

C

Tall
Sunflower

B

Common
Tansy

A

71

BROADLEAF SPRING BEAUTY
Claytonia caroliniana Michx.
Purslane family   Portulacaceae

woods   spring   6-10 in. (15-26 cm)

Usually 5-petaled pink or white flowers conspicuously marked with dark pink veins; style is 3-parted; there are 2 green sepals.

A single pair of smooth leaves halfway up the stem (rarely there may be 3 leaves), oval in shape, 1-3 in. (2-8 cm) long, with a definite leafstalk.

Leaves are thick and succulent.

Occurs primarily in the northern part of the state.

SPRING BEAUTY
Claytonia virginica L.
Purslane family   Portulacaceae

Distinguish from *C. caroliniana* by the much longer, 3-7 in. (7-18 cm) and narrower leaves that are stalkless, or nearly so. It is more apt to be found in the lower half of Michigan.

ROUND-LOBED HEPATICA or Liverleaf
Hepatica americana (DC.) Ker.
Crowfoot family   Ranunculaceae

woods   spring   4-6 in. (10-15 cm)

Delicate, pink, white, lavender, or blue flowers with 2-10 "petals."

Usually many individual flowers per plant, each with many threadlike stamens in its center, and each borne singly on a very hairy flowerstalk; 3 hairy bracts that resemble sepals below each blossom.

Leaves are smooth with 3 rounded lobes; leaves persist through the winter. At blossom time these overwintered leaves are present and have a brown-purple color. New green leaves develop after blossom time.

SHARP-LOBED HEPATICA   (not shown)
H. acutiloba DC.

Very similar to *H. americana* with these differences:
Leaf lobes are more pointed
Leaves are somewhat larger
Hairs on flowerstalk are longer
Leaves may have 3 or up to 7 lobes.

COLUMBINE or Rock Bells
Aquilegia canadensis L.
Crowfoot family   Ranunculaceae

dry woods, bogs, meadows
spring-early summer   up to 3 ft. (9 dm)

Flowers reddish with yellow centers, hanging or nodding at the end of a graceful, slender stem. The 5 petals have long tubes extending upward (or backward) into 5 curving spurs.

The basal leaves are long-stalked, divided and then divided again into segments of 3. Stem leaves are similar but are stalkless, decreasing in size toward the top of the plant. Leaflets are in 3's.

PLEASE DO NOT PICK

RED WINDFLOWER
Anemone multifida Poir.
Crowfoot family   Ranunculaceae

dunes   late spring-early summer
up to 12 in. (3 dm)

Flowers single, ¾-2 in. (2-5 cm) across, usually red (rarely purple, white, or yellow).

Basal leaves are long-stalked, deeply 3-parted into long, narrow segments. Stem leaves are similar but usually stalkless and occur near the middle of the stem.

Stems are stout, erect, and silky hairy.

Fruit appears as a tuft of cotton atop a long, dried stem.

INDIAN PAINTBRUSH or Painted Cup
Castilleja coccinea (L.) Spreng.
Figwort family   Scrophulariaceae

moist meadows, shores
spring-early fall   1-2 ft. (3-6 dm)

Conspicuous are the red, orange, or scarlet-tipped bracts that conceal the tiny, yellow or greenish true flowers.

Leaves are hairy; those on the stem may be entire (rare) but are usually deeply cleft into 3-5 narrow lobes. In either case the leaves are stalkless. Basal leaves form a rosette.

Stems are upright, often purple, and densely hairy. A parasite on other plants.

Broadleaf Spring Beauty   C

Columbine   C

Spring Beauty   C

Red
Windflower

C

Round-lobed Hepatica   C

Indian
Paintbrush

B

73

RAM'S-HEAD LADY'S-SLIPPER
Cypripedium arietinum R. Br.
Orchid family   Orchidaceae

woods, swamps, bogs   spring
6-12 in. (15-30 cm)

A single, nodding, pouch-like flower at top of stem. Pouch is conical, sagging on lower side, lined with fine hairs, and marked with darker color veins; pouch is white surmounted by a purplish hood.

Leaves are broad (up to 1 in. or 2.5 cm wide), long pointed, parallel veined, clasp the stem, and only 3-5 per stem; margins are entire.

A small plant difficult to find even though it often grows in colonies. The name comes from ram's-head appearance of the flower.

**PROTECTED MICHIGAN
WILDFLOWER—DO NOT DISTURB**

ARETHUSA or Dragon's Mouth
Arethusa bulbosa L.
Orchid family   Orchidaceae

swamps, bogs   late spring-early summer
6-12 in. (15-30 cm)

A solitary flower at tip of stem has 3 upright, pink sepals and a matching color hood over the lower lip, which is broad, purple spotted, and yellow bearded.

Stem is usually leafless at blossom time. Later, a single, narrow, grasslike leaf appears on the stem.

**PROTECTED MICHIGAN
WILDFLOWER—DO NOT DISTURB**

CALYPSO or Fairy Slipper
Calypso bulbosa (L.) Oakes
Orchid family   Orchidaceae

swamps, wet woods   late spring-
early summer   3-8 in. (8-20 cm)

A solitary pink to purple, nodding, slipper-shaped flower at tip of stem. Long, yellow hairs form the "laces" for the slipper. There are 2 yellow, pointed projections at "toe" of slipper.

Sepals and petals flare outward above the slipper. Dark lines and spots throughout the blossom.

A single, broad bladed, parallel veined leaf is at the base of the plant.

**A THREATENED SPECIES
DO NOT DISTURB**

SHOWY ORCHIS
Orchis spectabilis L.
Orchid family   Orchidaceae

woods   late spring   4-12 in. (10-30 cm)

Flowers are in an open spike of 3-8 bicolored blossoms; a broad, white lip below an arching pink to red-purple hood formed by sepals and side petals. Flowers have a green, leaflike bract at their base that is about the length of the blossom.

A pair of long (up to 7 in. or 18 cm), smooth, parallel veined leaves are at base of plant; leaves sheath the stem; margins smooth.

**PROTECTED MICHIGAN
WILDFLOWER—DO NOT DISTURB**

PINK LADY'S-SLIPPER or
Moccasin Flower
Cypripedium acaule Ait.
Orchid family   Orchidaceae

dry woods, swamps, bogs   late spring-
early summer   8-18 in. (20-46 cm)

Flower is a dark to very light, delicate pink; has a nodding, inflated pouch or "slipper" with conspicuously darker veins.

The 2 leaves (rarely 3) found at the ground line are very broad and have parallel veins. Both surfaces are hairy to downy.

One of the most common orchids. Often found in colonies.

**PROTECTED MICHIGAN
WILDFLOWER—DO NOT DISTURB**

ROSE POGONIA
Pogonia ophioglossoides (L.) Ker.
Orchid family   Orchidaceae

bogs, wet meadows   summer
4-20 in. (1-5 dm)

A solitary (rarely 2) flower(s) at tip of stem, pale to deep pink.

Sepals and petals are alike. The bearded and fringed lower lip is the most distinguishing characteristic along with the green, leaflike bract that occurs just below the flower.

A single leaf midway up the stem (may be 2-3) is long and comparatively narrow but too wide to be called grasslike. Base of leaf sheaths the stem.

**PROTECTED MICHIGAN
WILDFLOWER—DO NOT DISTURB**

Ram's-head
Lady's-slipper

D

Showy
Orchis

D

Arethusa

D

Pink
Lady's-slipper

C

Calypso

D

Rose
Pogonia

D

Red Trillium or Stinking Benjamin
Trillium erectum L.
Lily family   Liliaceae

woods   spring   6-24 in. (1.5-6 dm)

Flower color usually red to maroon but may vary to purple, yellow, greenish, or white; 1¼-2¾ in. (3-7 cm) across. The single flower is borne above the leaves and has an unpleasant odor. Sepals are about the same length as the petals.

Leaves are in a whorl, 3 in number.

Stems are upright with a single flower.

PROTECTED MICHIGAN WILDFLOWER—DO NOT DISTURB

Rose Twisted Stalk or Rose Mandarin
Streptopus roseus Michx.
Lily family   Liliaceae

woods   spring-early summer
1-2 ft. (3-6 dm)

Pink to rose-purple, bell-shaped flowers with 6 lobes, dangling singly on a bent or twisted, hairy flowerstalk that, in turn, arises from the stem at the leaf axil.

Leaves are stalkless, alternate, parallel veined, and have finely hairy margins.

Stem is arched and finely fuzzy.

Fruit is a globular, bright red berry.

White Twisted Stalk (not shown)
S. amplexifolius (L.) DC.

Similar to *S. roseus* but flowers are greenish-white or sometimes purple. Leaf bases clasp the stem. Fruit is an elongated, red berry.

Pale Corydalis
Corydalis sempervirens (L.) Pers.
Fumitory family   Fumariaceae

rocky meadows   spring-fall
6-24 in. (1.5-6 dm)

Open clusters of pink flowers with bright yellow tips occur at tip of stem; tube-shaped, ⅜-¾ in. (1-2 cm) in length with the flowerstalk attached at the side of the flower. 4 petals at the end of the tube.

Leaves are alternate, pinnately compound; leaflets mostly 3-lobed, ½ in. (13 mm) in length; lower leaves are stalked, upper are stalkless. Stems are both upright and prostrate; smooth.

Fruit is a long, narrow, bean-like pod.

Wild Geranium or Spotted Cranesbill
Geranium maculatum L.
Geranium family   Geraniaceae

woods, meadows   spring-early summer
1-2 ft. (3-6 dm)

Attractive pink, rose-purple, blue, or white flowers, singly or few flowered clusters at end of hairy flowerstalks. Flowers up to 1½ in. (4 cm) across. The 5 petals usually have dark lines (veins).

Leaves palmately compound, 3-5 lobes that are irregularly and coarsely toothed at their tips. Leaves are long-stalked at base of plant, shorter as they get higher on the stem.

Stems are hairy, erect, several to a plant.

Fruit is a long, thin pod resembling a crane's bill.

Herb-Robert or Red Robin
Geranium robertianum L.
Geranium family   Geraniaceae

woods and edges   late spring-summer
10-18 in. (26-46 cm)

Flowers are pink to reddish-purple (rarely white), approximately 12 mm across, with 5 petals that are prominently marked with dark-colored streaks. Flowers are usually in pairs on hairy flowerstalks.

Leaves are fernlike, deeply cut into 3-5 segments (leaflets) that, in turn, are deeply cleft.

Stems are erect and hairy, often reddish in color. Plant is strongly scented, the basis for a common name used in England, Stinking Bob.

Pitcher Plant
Sarracenia purpurea L.
Pitcher plant family   Sarraceniaceae

bogs, marshes, swamps   late spring-early summer   12-18 in. (3-5 dm)

Dark purple-red, single, nodding, globe-shaped flowers. There are 5 petals folded inward to form the globe.

Leaves are only at the base of the plant, tubular to urn-shaped, hollow, and usually contain water and dead insects. Color of leaves is variable from green to red with yellow stripes and blotches.

Stems are smooth, upright, leafless, and bent over at the tip from the weight of the blossom.

PLEASE DO NOT PICK

Red Trillium   D

Wild
Geranium

C

Rose Twisted Stalk   D

Herb-Robert   C

Pale Corydalis   C

Pitcher Plant

C

77

FRINGED POLYGALA or Gaywings
Polygala paucifolia   Willd.
Milkwort family   Polygalaceae

woods, swamps   late spring-early summer
3-6 in. (8-15 cm)

Petals form a tube tipped with a delicate fringe. A pink to purple "wing" is on each side of this tube. Blossoms resemble orchids but there is no relationship.

There are 3-6 oval leaves near the top of the stem with small, scalelike leaves on the lower stem. Stem is tough and woody.

SHOWY LADY'S-SLIPPER
Cypripedium reginae Walt.
Orchid family   Orchidaceae

swamps, bogs, wet woods   early summer
1-3 ft. (3-9 dm)

Flower is a pink and white ball-shaped pouch surmounted with widespreading white sepals and petals. May be up to 3 flowers on separate flowerstalks atop one single stem.

Leaves occur over the full length of the stem; are alternate, broad (up to 4 in. or 1 dm wide), veins parallel and prominent; upper and lower surfaces downy; bases clasp the stem.

Stems are erect and hairy. Plants often found in colonies.
PROTECTED MICHIGAN WILDFLOWER—DO NOT DISTURB

GRASS PINK
Calopogon pulchellus (Sw.) R. Br.
Orchid family   Orchidaceae

bogs, swamps, meadows   early summer
12-20 in. (3-5 dm)

An open cluster of pink to lavender, rarely white flowers that approximate 1 in. (2.5 cm) across. Petals and sepals mostly similar so blossoms appear to have 5 spreading "petals" and the exception is the single, upright, bearded "lip" at the top of the blossom. General appearance of the flower is an equal sided triangle.

There may be up to 12 blossoms per plant but usually 2-4.

A single, narrow, grasslike leaf from near the base of the plant, usually 4-8 in. (10-20 cm) long, upright (parallel with stem).
PROTECTED MICHIGAN WILDFLOWER—DO NOT DISTURB

RACEMED MILKWORT
Polygala polygama Walt.
Milkwort family   Polygalaceae

dry woods, meadows   summer
to 18 in. (4.5 dm)

Pink to rose-purple (seldom white) flowers in a loose spike at end of stems. Each flower with a central tube and 2 spreading wings similar to Fringed Polygala.

Leaves are simple, many, alternate, much longer than wide.

There are many stems from a common root; stems smooth, mostly upright but some tendency for outer stems to recline.

TWINFLOWER
Linnaea borealis L.
Honeysuckle family   Caprifoliaceae

wet woods, bogs   early summer
3-5 in. (8-13 cm)

Pale pink, nodding, elongated bell-shaped, fragrant flowers, ½ in. (13 mm) long, usually in pairs from the tip of the flower stalks, which are erect, usually 3-4 in. (8-10 cm) high.

Leaves are in pairs, essentially round, with some rounded teeth at the tip end; remain green year round.

Stems are woody and creep along the ground. Usually found in colonies that form mats.
PLEASE DO NOT PICK

EVERLASTING PEA
Lathyrus latifolius L.
Bean family   Fabaceae

meadows   late spring-summer
climber to 7 ft. (2 m)

Flowers pink, ranging from white to purple, resemble the cultivated sweet pea; 4-10 showy blossoms in a cluster near the tip of the smooth flowerstalk, which may be up to 7 in. (18 cm) long.

There are 2 leaflets from the end of each winged leafstalk. There may be one to several forked tendrils from the tip of the leafstalk. There is a pair of stipules (small leaflike appendages) at the base of each leafstalk, both 2-lobed, each lobe very narrow but one is much longer than the other.

Stems are climbing or prostrate. Stems are prominently winged like the leafstalks.

Fringed
Polygala

C

Racemed Milkwort   C

Showy
Lady's-slipper

C

Twinflower   D

Grass Pink

C

Everlasting Pea   B

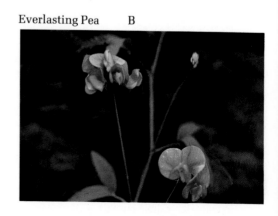

CROWN VETCH
Coronilla varia L.
Bean family   Fabaceae

meadows late spring-early fall   creeper*

Rounded clusters of clover-like, bicolored (pink and white) flowers on long stalks that arise in leaf axils.

Pinnately compound leaves with paired, oval leaflets, usually number 11, but may be up to 25.

*Stems are reclining or prostrate. A sprawling, many stemmed plant often planted to stabilize soil on steep slopes and road cuts.

Fruit is a long, slender pod.

BEACH PEA
Lathyrus maritimus (L.) Bigel.
Bean family   Fabaceae

dunes, sandy beaches summer
1-2 ft. (3-6 dm)

A cluster of 3-10 pea flowers on a long flowerstalk, each blossom ¾-1 in. (2-2.5 cm) long; range in color from a delicate pink through purple.

Leaves are pinnately compound with up to 6 pairs of egg-shaped leaflets. A pair of very large stipules is found at the base of the leafstalk. A forked tendril is at the tip of the leafstalk.

Stems are arching, climbing, or only somewhat erect, smooth, angled.

SMALL CRANBERRY
Vaccinium oxycoccos L.
Heath family   Ericaceae

bogs early summer creeping

Flowers have 4 flaring, backward curving, delicate pink lobes united at their base. Reproductive structures are compressed into a protruding, narrow column resembling a bird's beak. The 2-4 in. (5-10 cm) upright flowerstalks are red, fuzzy, and arise from the ends of the prostrate stems; there are usually 2 bracts below the middle of these upright stalks.

Leaves are alternate, pointed-oval in shape, up to ½ in. (1.3 cm) in length, whitish beneath, edges rolled inward.

Stems are reddish, prostrate, trailing, and woody.

Fruit is a rounded, red berry, ¼ in. (6-8 mm) in diameter. Edible but tart.

RED CLOVER
Trifolium pratense L.
Bean family   Fabaceae

meadows spring-fall to 24 in. (6 dm)

Deep purplish-red flowers form a globose, stalkless head at end of branches. Color may vary to almost white. Fragrant.

Leaves are palmately compound with 3 leaflets that usually have a V-shaped, lighter colored design on the blade. Leafstalks very hairy.

Stem is decidedly hairy. An important agricultural plant used for hay and pasture.

PIPSISSEWA or Prince's Pine
Chimaphila umbellata (L.) Bart.
Heath family   Ericaceae

dry woods summer 6-12 in. (15-30 cm)

Flowers are waxy, pale pink or white; spreading clusters nod from tip of stem; 2-8 blossoms per plant, each about ¾ in. (20 mm) across; 5 rounded and concave petals. A ring of red to rose-violet anthers surrounds the green center of the flower.

Leaves are in whorls, 2-3 tiers per stem; dark green, shiny on the upper surface, and sharply toothed along the margins; leaves remain green year-round.

PROTECTED MICHIGAN WILDFLOWER—DO NOT DISTURB

PINK PYROLA
Pyrola asarifolia Michx.
Heath family   Ericaceae

woods, swamps summer 6-12 in. (15-30 cm)

A spike of pink to pale purple, nodding, waxy, 5-petaled blossoms. Pistil exceeds length of the petals.

Leaves basal, kidney-shaped to round, leathery, often shiny. Length of leafstalk exceeds length of leaf blade.

Stem is essentially naked but has one or more scalelike bracts.

LARGE CRANBERRY (not shown)
Vaccinium macrocarpon Ait.

Similar to *V. oxycoccus* but somewhat larger; oval leaves are less pointed. Flowerstalks arise along the stem and from the tip. The pair of bracts on the flowerstalks are usually above the middle and are green. The plants grow in the same habitat and may be intermixed. The fruit of this species is grown commercially.

Crown Vetch　　　B

Red Clover　　　B

Beach Pea　　　C

Pipsissewa

D

Small Cranberry　　　D

Pink Pyrola

D

DAME'S ROCKET or Sweet Rocket
Hesperis matronalis L.
Mustard family   Cruciferae

meadows, wood edges
spring-midsummer   3-4 ft. (9-12 dm)

Open clusters of pink, white, or purple, 4-petaled, stalked flowers about 1 in. (2.5 cm) across; sepals hairy. Fragrant.

Leaves are alternate, short-stalked or stalkless, definitely not indented at the base; upper surface is finely downy, lower surface with branched hairs; margins may be smooth to undulating but more likely are finely toothed. Blade is 3-4 times longer than broad.

There may be one to many very hairy stems, hairiness increasing from top to bottom of stem.

Fruit is a long (up to 5 in. or 14 cm) cylindrical capsule.

HONESTY or Moonwort or Money Plant
Lunaria annua L.
Mustard family   Cruciferae

Another purple, sometimes white, 4-petaled flower of the Mustard family similar to *H. matronalis,* with these differences:

Stems are not as hairy, blooms earlier in the spring (fading about the time that Dame's Rocket is coming into bloom). Leaf blades are only about twice as long as broad, tapering to a point at the tip, are indented at their base, and are coarsely toothed. Most leaves are alternate but there may be some opposite leaves on the lower stem; very sparsely hairy on both surfaces. Fruits are round, flat, translucent disks about the size of a silver dollar. Popular in winter bouquets.

WILD BERGAMOT
Monarda fistulosa L.
Mint family   Labiatae

meadows   summer   2-4 ft. (6-12 dm)

Single clusters of tubular pink to lilac colored individual flowers that make a flower head at the tip of the stem. Each tubed flower has a tuft of long hairs at its tip.

Leaves are in pairs, short-stalked, longer than broad, widest below the midpoint, smooth to slightly hairy; margins are toothed.

Stems are also smooth to softly hairy, square in cross section (4-sided).

WILD THYME
Thymus serpyllum L.
Mint family   Labiatae

dry woods, meadows   summer
up to 12 in. (3 dm)

Flowers very small, pink to purple, form whorled clusters near the tip of the stem, appear to be 4-lobed. Calyx is green with white stripes, minutely hairy. Flowerstalks are short from upper leaf axils.

Leaves are paired, each leaf often with 2 small leaflike appendages at its base; margins are entire; minute pits are apparent on lower leaf surface.

Stems are 4-angled, finely fuzzy on the angles, mostly woody in the lower portion. Mostly prostrate, forming mats.

WILD BASIL or Dogmint
Satureja vulgaris (L.) Fritsch.
Mint family   Labiatae

wood edges, meadows   early summer-fall
9-18 in. (2-5 dm)

2-lipped, tubular, stalkless, pink to purple flowers in terminal clusters or in whorls in upper leaf axils. Flowers intermixed with many sharp pointed and densely hairy bracts.

Leaves opposite in pairs, deeply veined, egg-shaped with pointed ends, and hairy. Margins are smooth or shallow toothed.

Stems are hairy, 4-sided, upright; usually only a single stem per plant.

Not the basil of commerce.

MUSK MALLOW
Malva moschata L.
Mallow family   Malvaceae

meadows   summer   1-2 ft. (3-6 dm)

Large (1½-2 in. or 3-5 cm across), pink or white showy flowers; 5 wedge-shaped petals, notched at tips; a central core of bushy, pinkish stamens. There are about as many white flower forms as there are pink.

Leaves are palmately compound with (usually) 5 lobes deeply cut almost to the midrib; each lobe is itself deeply cut.

Stem is erect and hairy.

Fruit is a round, fuzzy disk surrounded by the 5 papery calyx lobes.

Dame's
Rocket

B

Wild Thyme   D

Honesty

C

Wild
Basil

C

Wild Bergamot   B

Musk Mallow   B

COMMON MILKWEED or Silkweed
Asclepias syriaca L.
Milkweed family   Asclepiadaceae

meadows, dunes   summer
2-4 ft. (8-12 dm)

Dusky pink to greenish-purple, fragrant flower clusters are dome or ball-shaped. What appears to be petals are cup-shaped structures, each surrounding a single, curved "horn." The 5 recurved petals (pointing backward along the stem) are immediately below this crown. Below the petals are 5 smaller, greenish sepals.

Leaves are thick, 4-6 in. (10-15 cm) long, softly hairy on the underside, oblong.

Stems are stout, hairy and, when cut or broken, exude a thick, milky juice.

Seed pods are long, pointed, covered with wartlike bumps. Seeds are tipped with long, silken hairs.

SWAMP MILKWEED
Asclepias incarnata L.
Milkweed family   Asclepiadaceae

wet meadows, swales   summer
3-4 ft. (9-12 dm)

Flowers are pink to purple, rarely white, in umbrellalike clusters at the top of the plant; many flowers on each plant; petals are recurved. Flowers fragrant.

Leaves are smooth, narrow; opposite in pairs.

Stems are stout, smooth to sparsely hairy, and have milky juice.

PLEASE DO NOT PICK

SPREADING DOGBANE
Apocynum androsaemifolium L.
Dogbane family   Apocynaceae

meadows, wood edges   summer
1-4 ft. (3-12 dm)

Usually pink but occasionally nearly white, fragrant flowers, bell-shaped with 5 spreading lobes that have deeper color stripes on their inner side.

Leaves are opposite and paired, smooth, egg-shaped with pointed tips; leafstalks very short; leaf margins smooth.

Stems are reddish and exude a milky juice. Larger stems have fibrous bark.

Fruit is an elongated pod that is round in cross section.

FIREWEED or Great Willow Herb
Epilobium angustifolium L.
Evening Primrose family   Onagraceae

meadows, swales summer-fall
3-5 ft. (9-15 dm)

Flowers have 4 rounded petals, pink or purplish-pink, form open clusters of conspicuous blossoms. The white stigma at the center of each flower is elongated and terminates in 4 lobes. There are 4 narrow, strap-like sepals between the petals.

Leaves are long, narrow, willowlike, smooth, and alternate.

Stems are erect, smooth, and often reddish color.

TEASEL
Dipsacus sylvestris Huds.
Teasel family   Dipsacaceae

meadows summer-fall   2-6 ft. (6-18 dm)

Flower head composed of many tiny, tubular, pink, white, or lavender florets interspersed between sharp pointed, slender bracts that are as long or longer than the florets. Immediately below the flower head are numerous, long (up to 4 in. or 1 dm), green, prickly bracts.

Leaves at base of plant are long (often up to 1 ft. or 30 cm or more) and wide (up to 2½ in. or 6 cm). Leaf surfaces are essentially smooth but scattered spines occur on upper leaf surface and the midrib on the under surface has a row of sharp, pointed spines. Leaves in pairs with bases that sheath the stem.

Stems are stout, rigidly upright, grooved, densely spiny in upper part.

Seed heads persist through the winter, often used in dried flower arrangements.

FIELD MILKWORT
Polygala sanguinea L.
Milkwort family   Polygalaceae

meadows, swamps summer
4-16 in. (1-4 dm)

A tightly packed cluster of rose-purple, white or greenish flowers at tip of stems, forming a short cylindric or round flowerhead.

Leaves are alternate along the stem, simple, stalkless, longer than wide; margins entire.

Stems are upright, single or branched, densely covered with leaves.

Common Milkweed   B

Fireweed

A

Swamp Milkweed   C

Teasel

B

Spreading Dogbane   C

Field Milkwort   C

Smooth or Meadow Rose
Rosa blanda Ait.
Rose family   Rosaceae

wood edges, dunes, meadows
summer   up to 3 ft. (9 dm)

Flowers conspicuous, up to 3 in. (5-7 cm) across, single or in few flowered clusters; 5 pink petals around a central yellow disk supporting numerous stamens.

Leaves are alternate, pinnately compound with 5-7 leaflets each on a short, smooth stalk; leaflets oval to oblong in shape; margins sawtoothed; leafstalks are winged and the stipules at the base of the leafstalks are broadest at their tips.

Upper stems are smooth and essentially thornless; lower stems may have a few slender thorns. A low shrub.

Fruit (hip) is dry, red, smooth, oval and not poisonous.

Swamp Rose   (not shown)
Rosa palustris Marsh.

Flower similar to *R. blanda*. Has many curved thorns; heights to 6 ft. and found in wetter habitats.

Mullein-Pink
Lychnis coronaria (L.) Desr.
Pink family   Caryophyllaceae

meadows   summer   1-3 ft. (3-9 dm)

Flowers have 5 crimson to deep rose color petals (rarely white); one or few flowers per plant. Calyx is tubular, strongly ribbed, and densely covered with long hairs.

Leaves are in pairs with 5-10 pairs along the stem; densely covered with whitish, wool-like hairs. Stems also woolly.

Sleepy Catchfly
Silene antirrhina L.
Pink family   Caryophyllaceae

meadows, dry woods   summer
8-30 in. (2-8 dm)

Small pink, sometimes white, upright flowers at tip of stem or lateral branches. Petals above an inflated base and do not last. Tips of calyx teeth usually dark red or purple.

Leaves are simple, opposite in pairs, long and narrow, and widely spaced along the stem. Margins are entire.

Stems are upright, minutely hairy at the bottom but smooth at the top. Also near the top are sticky bands in which insects may be trapped.

Corn Cockle or Purple Cockle
Agrostemma githago L.
Pink family   Caryophyllaceae

meadows   summer   1-3 ft. (3-9 dm)

A plant similar to *Lychnis coronaria* in respect to flower color, number of petals, shape and ribbing of the calyx, dense hairiness of calyx, leaves, and stems. The most noticeable difference is that this plant has flowers whose 5 calyx lobes greatly exceed the length of the petals, are narrow, and occur between the petals; leaves are much narrower.

Deptford Pink
Dianthus armeria L.
Pink family   Caryophyllaceae

meadows   summer   up to 20 in. (5 dm)

Pink to red flowers at tip of stems, up to ½ in. (1.25 cm) across. 5 wedge-shaped petals, white spotted, with rounded notches at tips. Calyx is white-striped, long and fuzzy. Narrow, pointed bracts arise from the base of the calyx and are at least as long as the calyx tube.

Leaves are narrow, linear, 1-2 in. (2.5-5 cm) long and up to ¼ in. (8 mm) wide, in pairs along the stem, and have clasping bases. Margins are entire and finely fuzzy.

Stem is mostly smooth but there is some hairiness at leaf joints.

Bouncing Bet or Soapwort
Saponaria officinalis L.
Pink family   Caryophyllaceae

meadows   summer-early fall
1-2 ft. (3-6 dm)

Open clusters of pink, white, or pinkish-white flowers with 5 heart-shaped petals. Base of blossom is a long, greenish tube.

Flowers are fragrant and have an overall ragged appearance. Leaves are opposite, 2-3 in. (5-8 cm) long and up to 1 in. (2.5 cm) wide, smooth, have a pointed tip, and veins are parallel.

Stems are coarse, upright, and smooth.

Plants usually found in colonies, especially on road shoulders.

Corn
Cockle

C

Smooth Rose   C

Mullein-
Pink

C

Deptford Pink   C

Sleepy
Catchfly

C

Bouncing
Bet

B

Bull Thistle
Cirsium vulgare (Savi) Tenore
Composite family   Compositae

meadows summer-fall up to 7 ft. (2 m)

Flower heads mostly single but may be as many as 3 at top of the stem; pink to reddish purple and with diameters up to 2 in. (5 cm). Stiff, yellow tipped spines cover the flower bracts. Only a few flower heads per plant (compared to Canada Thistle).

Leaves are deeply cut, the lobes coarsely toothed and tipped with a sharp pointed spine; leaf margins edged with shorter, prickly spines. Leaves "flow" into the stem and are persistently woolly on underside.

Stem is coarse, more or less hairy, and prominently covered with stout, exceedingly prickle-tipped wings.

Plant is more robust in every respect than *C. arvense*.

Canada Thistle
Cirsium arvense (L.) Scop.
Composite family   Compositae

meadows, swales summer-fall
3-5 ft. (9-15 dm)

Flowers are globular or flask-shaped, pink to rose-purple or even white (rare), ½-¾ in. (13-19 mm) across, and fragrant. Many flowers per plant.

Leaves alternate along the stem, are irregularly and deeply lobed and spiny-toothed; often woolly on underside of young leaves but become smooth and green on both surfaces of older leaves.

Stems are erect, grooved, and lack spines.

Spotted Knapweed or Spotted Star Thistle
Centaurea maculosa Lam.
Composite family   Compositae

meadows summer-fall 1-4 ft. (3-12 dm)

A shaggy blossom resembling Bachelor's Button of the cultivated garden to which it is related. Color is usually pink but may range from white to purple. Flowers are at the tips of the stems. Central part of the blossom consists of many individual, tubular flowers. The underpart of the flower head has overlapping, spiny, black-tipped bracts.

Stem leaves are few, deeply cut into narrow segments, are rough to the touch and grayish-green in color.

Stems are rough, wiry, and grayish-green.

Brown Knapweed
Centaurea jacea L.
Composite family   Compositae

meadows summer-fall 2-4 ft. (6-12 dm)

Flower color is pink to rose-purple. Bracts below the flower are light brown and appear to be outlined with a yellow-tan fringe. If bracts are removed from flower head, their tips have the appearance of having been irregularly torn rather than spiny-tipped (see Spotted Knapweed).

Leaves are alternate, irregularly and inconspicuously toothed (are not deeply cleft). Upper leaves are sessile (without stalks), lower leaves long-stalked and much larger than upper leaves.

Joe-Pye Weed or Spotted Joe-Pye Weed
Eupatorium maculatum L.
Composite family   Compositae

bogs, swales, stream banks
summer-fall 2-6 ft. (6-18 dm)

Flat-topped clusters of pink to purple flowers with 8-20 or more individual blossoms in each flower head.

Leaves are in whorls of 4-5, long, narrow, pointed at both ends, prominently veined, and with sawtooth margins.

Stem is blotched with purplish areas.

Cardinal-Flower
Lobelia cardinalis L.
Lobelia family   Lobeliaceae

meadows, swales summer-early fall
18 in.-5 ft. (4.5-15 dm)

Brilliant scarlet-red flowers on an upright spike, each blossom ¾-2 in. (2-5 cm) long. White forms occur but are very rare.

Leaves are thin, long, narrow, up to 6 in. (15 cm) long and 2 in. (5 cm) wide, with upper leaves much smaller than those lower on the plant. Leaf margins are minutely but visibly toothed.

Stems are upright, usually unbranched and usually smooth but may be slightly hairy.

One of the showiest of wildflowers.

PLEASE DO NOT PICK

Bull
Thistle

B

Brown
Knapweed

C

Canada
Thistle

B

Joe Pye Weed

B

Spotted
Knapweed

A

Cardinal-
flower

B

Bird-Foot Violet
Viola pedata L.
Violet family   Violaceae

dry woods   spring   3-6 in. (8-15 cm)

Lavender to blue flowers, ¾-1½ in. (2-4 cm) across; 5 petals, all beardless, lower one with a white spot at its base; nectar lines on this one petal only. Flowerstalks and leafstalks all come from base of plant. Flower is borne somewhat higher than the leaves.

Leaves are long stalked, deeply cleft into long, linear segments resembling a bird foot.

Often found in small clumps.

PROTECTED MICHIGAN WILDFLOWER—DO NOT DISTURB

Wild Ginger
Asarum canadense L.
Birthwort family   Aristolochiaceae

woods   spring   up to 10 in. (25 cm)

A single purple to red-brown flower, tubular at its base and flaring into 3 sharp pointed lobes that may be somewhat recurved (curving backwards). Flowerstalk is short, stout, and arises from between the 2 leaves. Calyx is hairy. There are no petals.

The 2 leaves are spreading, broadly heart-shaped, smooth on the upper surface but fuzzy on the lower; leafstalks are densely hairy; margins are entire. Contact with the leaves may cause a dermatitis on some susceptible people.

Jack-in-the-Pulpit or Indian Turnip
Arisaema triphyllum (L.) Schott.
Arum family   Araceae

swamps, bogs, woods   spring
1-3 ft. (3-9 dm)

Flowers are tiny, inconspicuous, hidden, borne at the base of the club-like "Jack." The canopy over the "Jack," and the "pulpit" are green or brownish-purple, often striped. Leaves 1-3, usually 2, each divided into 3 leaflets.

Stems are stout, upright, often mottled with purple and green, and have a sheathing membrane at the base.

Fruits are bright red berries in a tight cluster. Poisonous.

PLEASE DO NOT PICK

Wood Phlox
Phlox divaricata L.
Phlox family   Polemoniaceae

woods   spring-early summer
10-20 in. (2.5-5 dm)

Lavender to pale blue pinwheel-like flowers in a cluster radiate from tip of stem. Has 5 wedge-shaped petals that may be notched at their tips. Stamens hidden within the flower tube. Flowers are ¾-1¼ in. (2-3 cm) across.

Leaves are opposite, long and narrow, downy to somewhat hairy, tips blunt pointed; margins are entire; only a few leaves on a plant.

Stems are somewhat sticky and hairy.

Hairy Vetch
Vicia villosa Roth.
Bean family   Fabaceae

meadows   late spring-summer
2-3 ft. (6-9 dm)

Tightly packed clusters of miniature pea flowers strung along one side of the flowering spike; color is lavender to blue-violet or blue; bicolored.

Leaves are pinnately compound with 10-20 fuzzy leaflets; the central fuzzy leafstalk terminates in a threadlike tendril that may be branched. A pair of stipules at the base of leafstalk is hairy, shaped like half an arrowhead.

Stems are fuzzy, upright to reclining (mostly the latter).

Fruit is an elongated, flat pod.

Blue Cohosh or Papoose-Root
Caulophyllum thalictroides (L.) Michx.
Barberry family   Berberidaceae

woods   late spring   1-3 ft. (3-9 dm)

Flowers have 6 sharp pointed sepals that resemble petals and may be purple, brown, yellow-green, or greenish-yellow. The 6 petals are much smaller, are various shades of yellow, are found at the base of the sepals, and are hood-shaped. Each flower is up to ½ in. (1.3 cm) across and forms loose, terminal clusters.

Leaves are pinnately compound, 2 or 3 times subdivided; leaflets 2-5 with wedge-shaped bases and usually 3 (sometimes 5) pointed lobes. Leaflets resemble those of Meadow Rue.

Fruit is a cluster of paired, blue, berrylike seeds. All parts poisonous to eat.

Bird-foot
Violet

C

Wood
Phlox

B

Wild
Ginger

D

Hairy
Vetch

B

Jack-in-the-
pulpit

D

Blue Cohosh   D

Virginia Waterleaf
Hydrophyllum virginianum L.
Waterleaf family   Hydrophyllaceae

woods, swales   early summer
1-3 ft. (3-9 dm)

Open clusters of pale lavender to white flowers on long stalks usually well above the leaves. Each flower is funnel or bell-shaped with 5 stamens projecting well beyond the petals. Sepals are bristly.

Leaves are stalked, deeply cut almost to the midrib to form 5 lobes that are sharp pointed and coarsely toothed. Often have blotchy white markings resembling water marks.

Stem is smooth and weak.

Hound's Tongue
Cynoglossum officinale L.
Borage family   Boraginaceae

meadows, dunes   early summer
1-3 ft. (3-9 dm)

Reddish-purple or dull red flowers, nodding, bell-shaped with 5 rounded lobes, ⅜ in. (1 cm) across. Flowerstalks continue to elongate during flowering, reaching lengths of up to 8 in. (2 dm).

Lower leaves up to 12 in. (3 dm) long including the long winged leafstalk. Upper leaves progressively smaller than lower and shorter-stalked, ultimately stalkless. Leaves and stems velvety fuzzy. In fruit the 5 fuzzy calyx scales form a perfect star, cupping 4 flattened nutlets covered with hooked spines. Cling to clothing.

Butterwort
Pinguicula vulgaris L.
Bladderwort family   Lentibulariaceae

bogs, shores, wet areas   early summer
up to 8 in. (20 cm)

Flowers are pale lavender to reddish-purple, 5 petals and a spur, solitary at tip of flowerstalk. Somewhat resembles a violet (Viola) flower.

Leaves are distinctive, all basal, light yellow-green, greasy, edges rolled inward. Slimy substance coats leaves, which trap insects that are then digested by the plant.
PLEASE DO NOT PICK

Striped Coralroot
Corallorhiza striata Lindl.
Orchid family   Orchidaceae

woods   spring-early summer
up to 16 in. (4 dm)

Purple to reddish striped flowers in a spike of 10-20 blossoms. Individual flowers are drooping and up to 1¼ in. (31 mm) long. Plant appears to be leafless but 3-4 scalelike bracts can be found near the base of the stem. Plant is a saprophyte lacking chlorophyll so stems are various shades of purple, brown, or yellow rather than green. Often found in clumps.

Spotted Coralroot
Corallorhiza maculata Raf.
Orchid family   Orchidaceae

woods   summer   up to 20 in. (5 dm)

Similar to above but flowers are spotted rather than striped, blooms a bit later in the season, usually taller, often more flowers per spike (10-40) but these are smaller (up to ¼ in. or 2 cm long).

Northern or Early Coralroot
Corallorhiza trifida Chat. (not shown)

In contrast to the above species the flowers are white to yellow-green. Lip may be purple spotted. Blooms earlier (May) and is a smaller plant up to 12 in. or 30 cm. Stems are yellowish.

ALL CORALLORHIZAS ARE PROTECTED MICHIGAN WILDFLOWERS—DO NOT DISTURB

Self-Heal or Heal-All
Prunella vulgaris L.
Mint family   Labiatae

meadows, lawns   spring-fall
up to 12 in. (3 dm)

Flowers are 2-lipped, the upper lip hood-shaped and erect, the lower divided into 3 lobes, the 2 side lobes smaller than the central lobe, which is also fringed. Color is variable being lavender, blue, pink, or white. Flowers arise from between green, leafy bracts that are closely packed together to form a dense, often 4-sided column terminating the stem.

Leaves are opposite, elongate-oval, with margins that are entire to finely toothed.

Stems 4-sided, hairy to slightly fuzzy, erect or often reclining along the ground.

Virginia
Waterleaf

C

Striped
Coralroot

C

Hound's
Tongue

C

Spotted
Coralroot

C

Butterwort

C

Self-heal

C

Large-Leaved Aster
Aster macrophyllus L.
Composite family   Compositae

woods, wood edges   late summer
1-4 ft. (3-12 dm)

Open clusters of pale lavender, violet or white flowers at top of plant. Rays ("petals") 9-20 in number, from a central yellow disk that becomes reddish with age.

Lower leaves are long-stalked, large (4-8 in. or 10-20 cm wide), decreasing in size up the stem, surfaces rough to touch, margins with sawtooth edges. Upper leaves are stalkless.

There are large colonies of sterile (flowerless) plants consisting of the large, heart-shaped leaves while the flowering plants are few and scattered.

Smooth Aster
Aster laevis L.
Composite family   Compositae

meadows, dunes   late summer-fall
1-3 ft. (3-9 dm)

Flowers are showy and conspicuous, many per plant. Each flower has 15-20 "petals" that may be lavender, pale violet, blue, or white. Center of flower is yellow, becoming darker and even reddish as the flower ages.

Leaves are thick, variable in size and shape but longer than broad. Those on the upper stem become smaller, so small as to be mere bracts. Margins of upper leaves are entire, lower leaf margins sawtoothed. All leaf edges minutely hairy. Leaf bases clasp the stem.

Stem and leaf surfaces are smooth.

New England Aster
Aster novae-angliae L.
Composite family   Compositae

meadows   late summer-fall
3-7 feet. (9-21 dm)

The lavender to purple flowers are extremely showy because of their size (1-2 in. or 2.5-5 cm) and the vibrant color. There are from 45 to 100 "petals." The flower head is somewhat sticky.

Leaves and stem are conspicuously hairy.

Note: This aster prefers a moister habitat than *A. laevis* and the flowers are larger (flowers of Smooth Aster are seldom larger than ¾ in. or 2 cm across).

Rough Blazing Star
Liatris aspera Michx.
Composite family   Compositae

meadows   late summer   2-4 ft. (6-12 dm)

Many clusters of lavender to pink flower heads on a spike, short-stalked or stalkless from leaf axils. Ragged or feathery appearance is due to the projecting stamens.

Lower leaves are long, up to 14 in. (35 cm) counting the leafstalk, and up to 1¾ in. (4.5 cm) wide. Size decreases toward top of plant where leaves become sessile (stalkless). All leaves are thick, have smooth edges, and are covered with minute, white dots. Usually one stem covered with fine fuzz, bearing many leaves.

Common Burdock
Arctium minus   Schk.
Composite family   Compositae

meadows   summer-fall   2-6 ft. (6-18 dm)

Purplish to pink tubular florets atop a green, shiny bur, ½-1 in. (12-25 mm) wide, which is stalkless or short stalked from upper leaf axils.

Upper leaves are heart-shaped but without indentation, lower leaves larger than upper, leaves up to 1 ft. (3 dm) long or more are common; leafstalks are hollow; margins are wavy and minutely toothed.

The hooked barbs on the burs cling to clothing. Great Burdock, *Arctium lappa* L. (not shown) is a larger, more robust plant. The flowerstalks are longer, flower heads larger, and plant is taller, up to 8 ft. (24 dm).

Tick-Trefoil, Pointed Leaved
Desmodium glutinosum (Muhl.) Wood
Bean family   Fabaceae

dry woods   summer   1-4 ft. (3-12 dm)

Purple to pink pealike flowers rather sparsely spaced along a single or many branched hairy flowerstalk.

Leaves are compound with 3 leaflets; the 2 lateral leaflets are short-stalked or sessile, the terminal leaflet longer stalked and more sharply pointed. Blades about as broad as long. Leaves form a whorl from which the central flowerstalk arises.

Stem is erect and hairy. Fruits are flat, 3 jointed, roughly triangular pods covered with hooked hairs that cling to clothing.

Large-leaved
Aster

C

Rough
Blazing Star

B

Smooth
Aster

B

Common Burdock   C

New England
Aster

B

Tick-Trefoil

C

95

Marsh Thistle
Cirsium palustre (L.) Scop.
Composite family   Compositae

meadows, swales summer 1-7 ft. (3-20 dm)

Flower heads about ¾ in. (2 cm) across, uniformly purple, found in tight clusters at tip of stem; bracts are compressed against the flower head (not spreading) purple in color especially as maturity advances, are not spiny tipped, have a cobwebby appearance most noticeable just below the bracts.

Leaves are deeply cleft, strongly spiny, downy, webbed with hairs, and mostly on lower part of plant. Leaves on upper stem are fewer, smaller, and simpler.

Stem is spiny winged and hollow; stiffly upright.

Marsh Cinquefoil
Potentilla palustris (L.) Scop.
Rose family   Rosaceae

swamps, bogs, meadows   summer
1-2 ft. (3-6 dm)

The purple flowers are made of 2 rings of pet-allike structures. The true petals are smaller and immediately below them is a ring of larger (broader, longer) petallike sepals. Flowers are 1 in. (2.5 cm) across.

Leaves palmately compound with 5-7 leaflets; each leaflet is long and narrow and toothed along the margin.

Stems are hairy, stout, and upright

Hairy Beard-Tongue
Penstemon hirsutus (L.) Willd.
Snapdragon family   Scrophulariaceae

meadows, open woods summer
up to 3 ft. (1 m)

Tubular flowers up to 1 in. (2.5 cm) long, pale lavender with whitish tips, borne on long, hairy flowerstalks at tip of plant. One stamen is prominently yellow-bearded.

Leaves are simple, opposite, stalkless, long and narrow, and have sawtooth margins.

Stems are densely hairy, stiffly upright, usually purplish at the base, and often several per plant.

Purple Loosestrife or Spiked Loosestrife
Lythrum salicaria L.
Loosestrife family   Lythraceae

swales, swamps summer-fall
2-5 ft. (6-15 dm)

Reddish-purple flowers borne close together in a terminal spike; each flower has 6 petals but some may be found with 4, 5, or 7.

Leaves are narrow, long, up to 4 in. (10 cm), and usually opposite each other but occasionally may be single or in 3's.

Stems are stout, upright, ridged, usually smooth but may be somewhat fuzzy.

Plants occur in colonies, often covering sizable areas with their characteristic color.

Nightshade
Solanum dulcamara L.
Nightshade family   Solanaceae

swales summer-fall 2-12 ft. (6 dm-4 m)

Flowers with 5 purple to blue swept-back petals. There is a protruding yellow cone from the center of the blossom.

Leaves usually with 3 lobes; the oval shaped central lobe is large (1½-4 in. or 4-10 cm long) with 2 much smaller lobes at the base of the leaf. These 2 lobes may be absent from leaves on the lower stem.

Stems are woody at their base; hairy, weak, and twining in upper portion. Vines may climb to heights of 12 feet (4 m).

Fruit is an egg-shaped berry that hangs in clusters; red when ripe. The immature (green) berries and the foliage are poisonous. It is claimed that the ripe red berries are nontoxic; they have been used in cooking, but eating raw cannot be recommended.

Square-Stemmed Monkey Flower
Mimulus ringens L.
Figwort family   Scrophulariaceae

wet areas summer-early fall
up to 3 ft. (1 m)

Flowers are blue or sometimes violet, pink or white; about 1 in. (2.5-3 cm) long, solitary, on separate flowerstalks that are approximately double the length of the flower and are opposite in pairs from leaf axils.

Leaves are opposite, long and narrow, stalkless, and have sawtooth margins.

Stems are 4-sided and smooth.

Marsh
Thistle

B

Purple Loosestrife   A

Marsh
Cinquefoil

C

Nightshade

C

Hairy Beard-tongue   C

Square-stemmed Monkey Flower   C

97

Purple Fringed Orchid

Habenaria psycodes (L.) Spreng.
Orchid family   Orchidaceae

swamps, meadows summer
1-3 ft. (3-9 dm)

Flower head is a spike of fragrant, magenta, pink or light blue (rarely white) blossoms numbering up to 80 per spike; lower lip of each blossom is deeply cut into 3 fan-shaped segments, each of which is definitely fringed along its edge. Spike is up to 2 in. (5 cm) in diameter and 8 in (20 cm) in length.

Lower leaves are broad, parallel veined, and bases clasp the stem; upper leaves are much smaller.

**PROTECTED MICHIGAN
WILDFLOWER—DO NOT DISTURB**

Motherwort

Leonurus cardiaca L.
Mint family   Labiatae

wood edges summer to 5 ft. (15 dm)

Flowers small, 2-lipped from a tubular base, upper lip arched, lower with 3 lobes; interior of petals lavender to purple spotted or solid. Outside of upper lip is densely covered with white hairs. Flowers form whorls in leaf axils.

Leaves are in pairs, long stalked. Lower leaves with 3, long, sharp-pointed lobes at terminal end, each with a few sharp teeth; upper leaves simpler, smaller.

Stem is erect, stout, 4-sided, hairy on the upper part but smooth on lower portion.

Spearmint

Mentha spicata L.
Mint family   Labiatae

swales, meadows summer-fall
8-20 in. (2-5 dm)

Pale lavender to pink, tubed flowers with protruding stamens. Tiny individual blossoms in long, thin spikes at tips of the uppermost branches, formed in whorls in leaf axils (leaf size is greatly reduced in the blossom area). There is a short gap between clusters.

Leaves are in pairs and either stalkless or have very short stalks (3 mm or less); leaves are smooth, prominently veined; margins are toothed. Crushed leaves have a strong odor and taste of spearmint.

Stems are 4-sided and quite smooth.

Wild Mint

Mentha arvensis L.
Mint family   Labiatae

meadows summer-early fall
6-24 in. (1.5-6 dm)

Individual flowers are similar to preceding species. However, the clusters are spaced out along the stem in the leaf axils with a wide gap between clusters. Leaf size in the blossom area is not reduced. Flower color ranges from pale violet to lavender and (rarely) white.

Leaves are also similar to other two species and have a strong minty taste and odor.

Stem is fuzzy to hairy, 4-sided.

Peppermint

Mentha piperita L.
Mint family   Labiatae

meadows, streambanks
summer-early fall   1-3 ft. (3-9 dm)

Individual flowers similar to *M. spicata*. Flower spikes are thicker, shorter, and gaps between clusters much reduced.

Leaves are also similar, in pairs, have toothed margins, but the leafstalks are longer (4-15 mm), especially on larger leaves. Crushed leaves have a strong peppermint taste and odor.

Stems are smooth, 4-sided, and tend to be purple in color.

Blue-Eyed Mary

Collinsia verna Nutt.
Figwort family   Scrophulariaceae

woods, swales spring 8-16 in. (2-4 dm)

Bicolored flowers with a white upper lip and bright blue lower. 5 petals notched at tips; appear as 4 with a 5th petal folded lengthwise and hidden between the other 2 blue petals.

Lower leaves are broad to nearly round on long leafstalks. Upper leaves mostly long, narrow, stalkless, and in opposite pairs or in whorls. Margins coarsely toothed to entire.

Stems are single or many, smooth below and slightly hairy above; weak with many tending to recline.

This species is not widely distributed but where found forms brilliant, showy colonies, especially on wooded, river-bottom soils.

Purple
Fringed Orchid

C

Wild
Mint

D

Motherwort   D

Peppermint

C

Spearmint

C

Blue-Eyed Mary   C

LUPINE
Lupinus perennis L.
Bean family   Fabaceae

meadows   spring-early summer
1-2 ft. (3-6 dm)

Blue, blue-violet, pink or white pea flowers on short stalks from the central stem forming an open spike of blossoms; spike up to 10 in. (25 cm) long at tip of stem above the leaves.

Leaves are palmately compound with 7-11 leaflets, each 1-2 in. (2-5 cm) long.

Stems are erect, fuzzy, usually many branched.

Fruit is a hairy, elongated pod.

GARDEN LUPINE
Lupinus polyphyllus Lindl.
Bean family   Fabaceae

meadows   summer   2-4 ft. (6-12 dm)

Extremely showy spikes of large blue, violet, pink, or white, pea flowers closely packed along a central stem at top of plant; flower spike is up to 18 in. (4.5 dm) long.

Leaves are palmately compound with 12-18 leaflets.

A garden escape, larger and showier than *L. perennis*. Found primarily in the Keweenaw Peninsula and south into the western counties of the Upper Peninsula.

COMMON BLUE VIOLET
Viola papilionacea Pursh.
Violet family   Violaceae

woods, meadows   spring   3-8 in. (8-20 cm)

The 5-petaled flowers are blue to light or dark purple, the lower petal smooth and extending backward into a short spur; the 2 side petals are bearded, and all 3 have strongly contrasting veins (nectar lines).

Leaves are broadly heart-shaped with coarse, round toothed margins; smooth leafstalks may be up to 5 in. (13 cm) long.

This is one of the "stemless" violet group with both the leafstalks and flowerstalks arising from a buried rhizome or underground stem.

Violets hybridize freely, causing countless variations.

BLUE IRIS or Blue Flag
Iris versicolor L.
Iris family   Iridaceae

swales, swamps   late spring-early summer
2-3 ft. (6-9 dm)

Blossoms consist of petals and sepals that are both of the same general color, sepals are widespreading and marked at the base with a greenish-yellow or yellow blotch; petals stand upright, are ½-⅔ the length of the sepals. Both the petals and the sepals are strongly marked with darker colored veins.

Leaves are long and narrow resembling the blade of a sword, arise mainly from the base of the plant.

DWARF LAKE IRIS
Iris lacustris Nutt.
Iris family   Iridaceae

beaches, bogs   late spring
less than 8 in. (2 dm)

Structure of flower is similar to *I. versicolor*. Flower is about 2" (5 cm) across.

Leaves are flat, ½ in. (1.3 cm) broad and 3-6 in. (8-15 cm) long at blossom time but later grow to a length of up to 8 in. (20 cm). This is a miniature iris plant found almost exclusively on the sandy or gravelly shores of Lakes Michigan and Huron and in marshy or boggy areas adjacent.

Usually found in colonies.

A THREATENED SPECIES
DO NOT DISTURB

BLUE-EYED GRASS
Sisyrinchium albidum Raf.
Iris family   Iridaceae

meadows, swales   spring
6-18 in. (1.5-4.5 dm)

The "eye" of blue-eyed grass is yellow. The 3 petals and 3 sepals are identical in appearance and each sharply pointed at its tip. The flower is exceeded by a sharp-pointed bract that terminates the stem.

Leaves are flat, narrow (3 mm), grasslike, arise from base of plant, sharply folded at the base, and pointed at tips.

Stems are stiff, erect, winged on 2 sides, making stem appear flat.

Lupine

B

Blue Iris　　　B

Garden
Lupine

B

Dwarf Lake Iris　　　C

Blue-
Eyed grass

D

Common Blue Violet　　　C

HAREBELL or Bluebell
Campanula rotundifolia L.
Harebell family   Campanulaceae

dunes, meadows spring-summer
12-18 in. (3-4.5 dm)

Bell-shaped flowers with 5-pointed lobes, nodding at the end of thin, wiry stems. Color is usually blue but may be pink or white.

Basal leaves are long-stalked, roundish, and tend to dry up and disappear before the flowers appear. Stem leaves are long and narrow, up to 4 in. (10 cm) in length.

PERIWINKLE or Myrtle
Vinca minor L.
Dogbane family   Apocynaceae

woods spring-summer *see below

A 5-petaled blue flower up to 1 in. (2.5 cm) across, on short, erect stemlets, rising above the uppermost 2 pairs of leaves. A white, 5-pointed star is outlined in the center of the blossom. Petals are blunt tipped.

Leathery, shiny leaves in pairs along the stem remain green year around.

*Smooth stems recline along the ground, vine-like, up to 3 ft. (1 m) long, forming mats that may cover large areas. This plant is a garden escape and often found in the vicinity of old or abandoned homesteads, cemeteries, and along roadsides.

COMMON SPEEDWELL
Veronica officinalis L.
Figwort family   Scrophulariaceae

woods, meadows, lawns spring-fall
prostrate

4-petaled pale blue or lavender flowers. There are 3 spreading, somewhat rounded petals, the 4th petal being distinctly smaller; a pair of projecting stamens. Flowers ¼ in. (6 mm) across, sparsely distributed along an up-turned flowerstalk that arises from the prostrate, hairy stem.

Leaves mostly oval with a wedge-shaped base, up to 2 in. (5 cm) long; margins are sharp toothed.

Stems root from the nodes.

FORGET-ME-NOT
Myosotis scorpioides L.
Borage family   Boraginaceae

swamps, moist areas spring-fall
6-24 in. (1.5-6 dm)

Flowers are small, up to ¼ in. (6 mm) across, very pale blue or white (rarely pink); 5 rounded petals; center of flower is yellow with 5 starlike points. The stemlets bearing the flowers tend to uncoil as the blossoms open.

Leaves are stalkless, longer than broad, hairy, and alternate along the stem.

Stems are hairy, upright in young plants but later are more or less prostrate along the ground.

Usually in colonies forming a showy mat of blossoms.

BLUEWEED or Viper's Bugloss
Echium vulgare L.
Borage family   Boraginaceae

meadows summer-early fall
2-3 ft. (6-9 dm)

Bright blue to violet-blue flowers on short, curved stalks from the main stem. Prominent, long red stamens project beyond the petals. Flower buds are pink. Flowers are sometimes white or pink.

Leaves are long, narrow, and very hairy on both surfaces so leaves feel velvety.

Stems have many small, brownish dots from which bristly spines arise. Entire plant is conspicuously bristly-hairy.

PICKERELWEED
Pontederia cordata L.
Pickerelweed family   Pontederiaceae

shallow water, ponds summer-fall
1-3 ft. (3-9 dm)*

Tiny blue flowers on narrow spikes, the flowering portion being up to 4 in. (10 cm) long. Each flower is 2-lipped with each lip 3-lobed.

Leaves are smooth, broad, heart-shaped; with a deep indentation at the base.

Plants grow partially submerged in shallow water, usually in colonies.

*This is the height above the surface of the water.

Harebell   C

Forget-me-not   C

Periwinkle   C

Blueweed

B

Common Speedwell   D

Pickerelweed   C

103

CHICORY or Blue Sailors
Cichorium intybus L.
Composite family   Compositae

meadows summer-fall up to 5 ft. (15 dm)

Showy flowers that are almost always blue but in rare cases might be white or pink. Petals are blunt and fringed at the tip.

Blossoms are stalkless, attached directly to the main stem.

The basal leaves are dandelion-like, the margins having jagged, sharp-pointed lobes. Leaves on the stem are few and small, especially on the upper stem. Upper and lower leaf surfaces are hairy with longer hairs on the lower side of the midrib. Stem leaves clasp the stem with sharp pointed projections.

Stems are wiry, tough, shallow grooved, and sparsely to densely covered with weak spines.

COMMON SKULLCAP or Marsh Skullcap
Scutellaria galericulata L.
Mint family   Labiatae

swamps, shores, meadows summer-fall
up to 30 in. (7.6 dm)

Blue, violet-blue, pink, or white flowers borne singly or in pairs in leaf-axils ¾-1 in. (2-2.5 cm) in length on very short flowerstalks; tubular at base flaring into 2 lips, the upper one of which is hooded, forming the "skullcap."

Leaves are opposite in pairs, very short stalked or stalkless, long, narrow with pointed tips; margins slightly toothed; lower leaf surface often fuzzy, upper surface less so.

Stems square in cross section, erect, hairy.

BLUE VERVAIN
Verbena hastata L.
Vervain family   Verbenaceae

meadows, swales, marshes
summer-early fall 18 in.-5 ft. (4.5-15 dm)

The single stem terminates in a many branched flower head of individual spikes, each spike bearing a cluster of small, blue to violet-blue colored flowers, each with 5 petals. Flowering commences at the base of each spike and progresses upward.

Leaves are opposite, long, narrow, pointed, and toothed along the margins.

Stems are 4-sided, erect, and covered with short hairs.

GREAT LOBELIA
Lobelia siphilitica L.
Lobelia family   Lobeliaceae

meadows, swamps, shores
late summer-fall 1-3 ft. (3-9 dm)

Blue, tubular flowers flaring into 2 lobes at top of blossom and 3 wider lobes at the bottom. Lower lobes are streaked with white.

Flowers are up to 1 in. (2.5 cm) long, borne singly on short spikelets; the several individual flowers together form a wide, conspicuous spike.

Leaves are thin, long, 3-5 in. (8-13 cm), narrow, stalkless, and have finely toothed margins. Stems are stout, erect, smooth or very slightly hairy.

PLEASE DO NOT PICK

FRINGED GENTIAN
Gentiana crinita Froel.
Gentian family   Gentianaceae

woods, meadows, swales late summer-fall
1-3 ft. (3-9 dm)

Showy, bright blue or violet (rarely white) flowers with 4 conspicuously fringed petals that arise from a tubed base. A single flower surmounts each stem. Blossoms often close at evening and on cloudy days.

Leaves are paired, stalkless, smooth margined, and smaller than Closed Gentian.

**PROTECTED MICHIGAN
WILDFLOWER—DO NOT DISTURB**

CLOSED GENTIAN or Bottle Gentian
Gentiana andrewsii Griseb.
Gentian family   Gentianaceae

woods, meadows, swales
late summer-fall 18 in.-3 ft. (4.5-9 dm)

Flowers are blue, violet, or white in upright clusters of egg-shaped blossoms at tip of stem or in upper leaf axils. Blossoms remain closed or nearly so and are tipped with a minute, whitish fringe.

Leaves are in pairs, opposite, stalkless, and have smooth margins; are 1½ in. (4 cm) long in width and up to 6 in. (15 cm) long, veins parallel.

**PROTECTED MICHIGAN
WILDFLOWER—DO NOT DISTURB**

Great
Lobelia

C

Chicory   B

Common
Skullcap

D

Fringed Gentian   C

Blue
Vervain

B

Closed Gentian   C

Skunk Cabbage

Symplocarpus foetidus (L.) Nutt.
Arum family   Araceae

swamps, springy areas   early spring
up to 5 in. (13 cm)*

The stemless flower structure is at ground level. It has a shell-like, mottled hood of green to purple or purple-brown, up to 5 in. (13 cm) tall, with rolled edges. The knob in the center of this shelter bears the tiny, yellow flowers.

At blossom time leaf development is just beginning and may not yet be visible or may be tightly inrolled around the flower structure.

*Later in the season the leaves become very large, up to 2 ft. (6 dm) long, and broad, somewhat heart-shaped, and have leafstalks that are green, grooved, and succulent; margins smooth to wavy.

Seaside Arrow-Grass

Triglochin maritima L.
Arrow-Grass family   Juncaginaceae

shores, bogs, swamps   spring
up to 30 in. (7.5 dm)

Tiny greenish flowers on a very narrow spike on upper half of flowerstalk, often many flowerstalks per plant.

Flowerstalks and leaves arise separately from ground level.

Leaves all basal, upright, grasslike, fleshy, shorter than the flowering spike.

Common Cattail

Typha latifolia L.
Cattail family   Typhaceae

wet open areas   spring, summer
3-9 ft. (1-3 m)

Hundred of tiny, brown flowers without petals or sepals, so closely crowded together as to form a compact mass resembling a hot dog at the tip of the stem. The female flowers are separate from the male flowers, being at the bottom of the spike, the male flowers just above. There is no gap (or possibly a very slight one) between the two sexes.

Leaves are swordlike, ½ in. or more wide (1.25 cm), are flat with leaf bases clasping the stem.

The related Narrow-Leaved Cattail, *T. angustifolia* L. (not shown) is not as tall, flower spikes are thinner, leaves narrower (not exceeding ½ in. wide), and there is usually a definite gap between the male and female flowers.

Spurred Gentian

Halenia deflexa (Sm.) Griseb.
Gentian family   Gentianaceae

bogs, marshes, wet woods   summer
6-30 in. (1.5-8 dm)

4-petaled, greenish, bronze, or purplish flowers in a cluster at tip of stem or from upper leaf axils; cone-shaped with 4 projecting spurs from the rear.

Leaves are opposite, oval to elongated, egg-shaped, narrowing to pointed tips; upper leaves stalkless (sessile), lower with short leafstalks; margins are entire.

Stems are upright, twisted, smooth.

PROTECTED MICHIGAN WILDFLOWER—DO NOT DISTURB

Curled Dock or Sour Dock

Rumex crispus L.
Smartweed family   Polygonaceae

meadows   summer-fall   1-4 ft. (3-12 dm)

Small green or reddish-brown, inconspicuous flowers 1-3 mm across, in whorls on flowerstalks from leaf axils.

Leaves are long, up to 1 ft. (3 dm), and relatively narrow; strongly veined; wavy leaf margins.

Stems erect, smooth, ridged, green to brown. Fruits reddish-brown to brown, small, winged seeds, only 1-3 mm across, conspicuous because of their large number and color. Photo shows the seeds.

Ground Nut or Indian Potato

Apios americana Medicus
Bean family   Fabaceae

shores, swales   summer   vine

Brown (also reddish to maroon) color, fragrant, pealike flowers form short, rather dense clusters at end of long flowerstalks that arise in leaf axils.

Leaves are pinnately compound with 5-7 egg-shaped but sharp-pointed leaflets.

Stems are short, climbing vines with milky juice. Rhizome is thickened at intervals to form small tubers (resembles a necklace). Edible.

Skunk
Cabbage

D

Spurred
Gentian

C

Seaside
Arrow-grass

D

Curled
Dock

D

Common
Cat-tail

B

Ground Nut   C

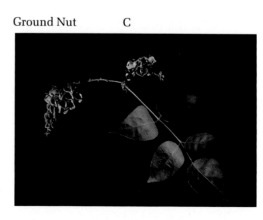

HELLEBORINE

Epipactis helleborine (L.) Crantz.
Orchid family   Orchidaceae

woods   summer   1-3 ft. (3-9 dm)

Terminal spikes of nodding flowers, each with a green calyx tube, ridged and as long as or longer than the purple petals and sepals; each flower from the axil of a long, narrow, leafy bract.

Leaves are alternate, long, narrow, smooth; upper leaves stalkless to very short-stalked while the lower leaves clasp the stem; veins are prominent and parallel; margins entire and finely fuzzy.

Stem is erect, downy, and purplish.

**THIS AND THE FOLLOWING TWO
ORCHIDS ARE PROTECTED
MICHIGAN WILDFLOWERS
DO NOT DISTURB**

HEARTLEAF TWAYBLADE

Listera cordata (L.) R.Br.
Orchid family   Orchidaceae

wet woods, bogs, swamps   early summer
3-10 in. (7-25 cm)

Flowers are small (4-5 mm long), strung along an upright spike; green, purplish-green, tan or dark purple; lower lip is longer than the other petals and is forked and spreading.

There is a single pair of heart-shaped, stalkless leaves opposite each other below the middle of the stem.

Stem is smooth except in the area of the flowers.

TALL NORTHERN BOG ORCHID

Habenaria hyperborea (L.)   R.Br.
Orchid family   Orchidaceae

bogs, wet woods, swamps   summer
6-40 in. (1.5-10 dm)

Usually dense but sometimes loose spikes of green to yellow-green flowers. Lower lip is relatively long, narrow, and pointed. A projecting spur is about the same length as the lower lip. The green floral bracts are longer than the flowers at the bottom of the spike, but become progressively shorter toward the top.

There are many leaves, some up to 8 in. (2 dm) long. Parallel veined, bases wrapped around the stem; shiny, smooth.

Stem is stout and stiffly upright.

RAGWEED

Ambrosia artemisiifolia L.
Composite family   Compositae

meadows, fields, waste areas
summer-fall   up to 4 ft. (1.2 m)

The inconspicuous green flowers are either male or female but not both and occur on the same plant. Male flowers are many, borne in spikes at the tips of the stems, are saucer shaped, downward facing, and can be loaded with yellow pollen. Female flowers are fewer, occur below the male flowers in the upper leaf axils and forks of branching stems.

Leaves are mostly smooth, deeply cut into many lobes, each lobe is deeply cut.

Stems are upright and usually hairy. The pollen from these plants is the primary contributor to hay fever allergies.

TALL WORMWOOD

Artemisia campestris L.
Composite family   Compositae

dunes, dry sand   summer-fall
2-5 ft. (6-15 dm)

Large numbers of tiny, globular, nodding, green to yellow flowers loosely arranged along many short, upward pointed side branches.

Leaves are very finely dissected, almost stringlike, aromatic, gray-green.

Usually a single stem plant; stem is smooth.

Somewhat resembles ragweed some individuals are allergic to its pollen.

CYPRESS SPURGE

Euphorbia cyparissias L.
Spurge family   Euphorbiaceae

meadows   spring-summer
8-16 in. (2-4 dm)

Compare with Leafy Spurge (p. 62). There are these differences:

In Cypress Spurge, bracts of flowerhead, yellowish-green turning to reddish or purplish, are smaller and more broadly rounded. Plants are smaller. Leaves are very narrow and shorter, 1 in. (2.5 cm) or less, even more numerous, very crowded on upper stem.

Like Leafy Spurge, the stems are erect and contain milky juice. Plants often form colonies, frequently in and around cemeteries.

Helleborine

D

Ragweed

C

Heartleaf
Twayblade

D

Tall
Wormwood

C

Tall Northern
Bog Orchid

D

Cypress
Spurge

C

Quiz Section
Test Your Flower Power!

Individual plants have their own special beauty and become a striking display when growing in masses or mixed with other species. The challenge is to identify the individual blossom. Ignore the flowers that are indistinct and name the predominating ones in each picture. You will find a helpful hint beside each photograph. Good Luck!

To confirm your answers and check your rating, see page 114.

A Two of Michigan's protected wild-flowers found in late summer in meadows, woods, and on shores.

B

This conspicuous yellow flower with a blackish-brown disk is shown growing with a white daisy-like blossom.

C

A lacelike member of the parsley family found in meadows and on roadsides in the summer and fall.

D

Note the four petals. This plant can be a serious pest in farmers' fields and on land that is no longer being farmed.

A

Usually found in damp to wet areas including open woods in early spring.

B

Another popular garden flower that has escaped into the wild. A summer flower found in dry, open woods, meadows, and even sand dunes.

C

A better view of the yellow flower found on the preceding page. Also name the small white flower that often grows so thickly it forms mats.

D

One of the showiest, hardiest, and widespread of all our wildflowers. Found lining the roadsides from summer to autumn.

A

The rounded clusters of pea-like flowers grow on stems that become tangled mats, thus are good for stopping soil erosion of bare areas.

B

Everybody recognizes the yellow-flowered plant. A clue to identifying the pink one—its genus is *Eupatorium.*

C

Not always does this plant grow under such harsh conditions; it usually grows in meadows that are not so hostile. The white flower on the left is another hardy plant.

D

You will find this plant growing in moist, shady places in spring and early summer.

A

Of the three species illustrated here, one is related to a medium-sized shrub and one is an endangered species found in northern Michigan on rocky shores and in cedar swamps. The third is sometimes mistakenly thought to be a member of the Orchid family.

B

First find the tall, slender plants with yellow blossoms; then name the orange colored flowers that hang like jewels in the background on the left. Finally, identify the tall, slender pink spikes that environmentalists are trying to eradicate.

C

These two species are sharing a moist site such as found in a thicket, swale, or lakeshore.

D

Two of the most prominent fall wildflowers of open fields and roadsides.

Answers to Quiz Section

Check Your Flower Power Here

Pg 110 **A** Common or Nodding
Ladies'- Tresses
Spiranthes cernua

Fringed Gentian
Gentiana crinita

B Black-Eyed Susan
Rudbeckia hirta

Fleabane
Erigeron strigosus

C Wild Carrot or
Queen Anne's Lace
Daucus carota

D Yellow Rocket or
Winter Cress
Barbarea vulgaris

Pg 111 **A** Golden Alexanders
Zizia aurea

B Coreopsis
Coreopsis lanceolata

C Coreopsis
Coreopsis lanceolata

Rock Sandwort
Arenaria stricta

D Ox-Eye Daisy
*Chrysanthemum
leucanthemum*

Pg 112 **A** Crown Vetch
Coronilla varia

Pg 112 **B** Joe-Pye Weed
Eupatorium maculatum

Canada Goldenrod
Solidago canadensis

C Smoothish Hawkweed
Hieracium floribundum

D Clintonia
Clintonia borealis

Pg 113 **A** Bunchberry
Cornus canadensis

Fringed Polygala
Polygala paucifolia

Dwarf Lake Iris
Iris lacustris

B Purple Loosestrife
Lythrum salicaria

Mullein
Verbascum thapsus

Joe-Pye Weed
Eupatorium maculatum

C Boneset
Eupatorium perfoliatum

Cardinal-Flower
Lobelia cardinalis

D Canada Goldenrod
Solidago canadensis

New England Aster
Aster novae-angliae

Score 1 point for each flower identified correctly, 26 possible points.

13-17 correct	***Good***
18-22 correct	***Excellent***
23-26 correct	***Exceptional***

OBSERVER'S LIST	seen by			date	location
Agrimony					
Alyssum					
Anemone, Canada					
Anemone, False Rue					
Anemone, Rue					
Anemone, Wood					
Arbutus, Trailing					
Arethusa					
Arrow-Grass, Seaside					
Asphodel, Sticky False					
Aster, Flat-Topped					
Aster, Large-Leaved					
Aster, New England					
Aster, Smooth					
Baneberry, Red					
Baneberry, White					
Basil, Wild					
Bearberry					
Beard-Tongue, Hairy					
Bellwort, Large-Flowered					
Bergamot, Wild					
Betony, Wood					
Bindweed, Field					
Birdsfoot Trefoil					
Black-Eyed Susan					
Blazing Star, Rough					
Bloodroot					
Blue-Eyed Grass					
Blue-Eyed Mary					
Blueweed					
Boneset					
Bouncing Bet					
Broom-Rape, Clustered					
Buckbean					
Bunchberry					

Observer's List (cont.)	seen by			date	location
Burdock, Common					
Burdock, Great					
Butter-and-Eggs					
Buttercup					
Butterfly Weed					
Butterwort					
Calypso					
Campion, Bladder					
Campion, White					
Cardinal-Flower					
Carrot, Wild					
Catnip					
Cattail, Common					
Cattail, Narrow-Leaved					
Chamomile, Scentless					
Checkerberry					
Cherry, Ground					
Chicory					
Cinquefoil, Marsh					
Cinquefoil, Sulfur					
Cinquefoil, Three-Toothed					
Clintonia					
Clover, Red					
Cockle, Corn					
Cohosh, Blue					
Columbine					
Comandra, Northern					
Coneflower, Tall					
Coralroot, Northern or Early					
Coralroot, Spotted					
Coralroot, Striped					
Coreopsis					
Corydalis, Pale					
Cow Wheat					
Cranberry, Large					

Observer's List (cont.)	seen by			date	location
Cranberry, Small					
Cress, Spring					
Cucumber-Root, Indian					
Cucumber, Wild					
Culver's Root					
Daisy, Ox-Eye					
Dame's Rocket					
Dandelion, Common					
Dock, Curled					
Dogbane, Spreading					
Dogfennel					
Dutchman's Breeches					
Everlasting, Pearly					
Fireweed					
Fleabane					
Foamflower					
Forget-Me-Not					
Gentian, Closed					
Gentian, Fringed					
Gentian, Spurred					
Geranium, Wild					
Ginger, Wild					
Ginseng, Dwarf					
Goat's-Beard					
Goat's Beard, Purple					
Goat's Rue					
Golden Alexanders					
Goldenrod, Bluestem					
Goldenrod, Canada					
Goldthread					
Grass Pink					
Grass-of-Parnassus					
Grass-of-Parnassus, Small					
Greenbrier					
Ground Nut					

Observer's List (cont.)	seen by			date	location
Harebell					
Hawkweed, Field or Yellow					
Hawkweed, Orange					
Hawkweed, Smoothish					
Heal-All					
Heather, False					
Helleborine					
Hepatica, Round-Lobed					
Hepatica, Sharp-Lobed					
Herb-Robert					
Honesty					
Horehound, Cut-Leaved Water					
Horsemint					
Hound's Tongue					
Indian Paintbrush					
Indian Pipe					
Indigo, Prairie False					
Iris, Blue					
Iris, Dwarf Lake					
Jack-in-the-Pulpit					
Jewelweed, Spotted					
Joe-Pye Weed					
King Devil					
Knapweed, Brown					
Knapweed, Spotted					
Ladies' Tresses, Common					
Lady's -Slipper, Ram's-Head					
Lady's-Slipper, Pink					
Lady's-Slipper, Showy					
Lady's-Slipper, Yellow					
Lettuce, White					
Lily, Day					
Lily, Dune					
Lily, Fawn					
Lily, Michigan					

Observer's List (cont.)	seen by			date	location
Lily, Wood					
Lily, Yellow Trout					
Lily-of-the-Valley, Wild					
Lobelia, Great					
Loosestrife, Purple					
Loosestrife, Tufted					
Lupine					
Lupine, Garden					
Mallow, Musk					
Marigold, Marsh					
May Apple					
Meadow-Rue, Early					
Meadow-Rue, Purple					
Meadowsweet					
Milkweed, Common					
Milkweed, Swamp					
Milkwort, Field					
Milkwort, Racemed					
Mint, Wild					
Mitrewort					
Mitrewort, Naked					
Moneywort					
Monkey Flower, Square-Stem					
Motherwort					
Mullein, Common					
Mullein, Moth					
Mullein-Pink					
Nightshade					
Nightshade, Enchanter's					
Orchid, Purple Fringed					
Orchid, Tall Northern Bog					
Painted Cup, Pale					
Parsnip, Cow					
Parsnip, Water					
Parsnip, Wild					

Observer's List (cont.)	seen by			date	location
Partridgeberry					
Pea, Beach					
Pea, Everlasting					
Peppermint					
Periwinkle					
Phlox, Wood					
Pickerelweed					
Pimpernel, Yellow					
Pinesap					
Pink, Deptford					
Pipsissewa					
Pitcher Plant					
Pogonia, Rose					
Poison Ivy					
Polygala, Fringed					
Pondlily, Yellow					
Primrose, Birdseye					
Primrose, Evening					
Puccoon, Hairy					
Puccoon, Hoary					
Pyrola, Pink					
Ragweed					
Ragwort, Golden					
Rock Cress, Lyre-Leaved					
Rock Sandwort					
Rose, Smooth					
Rose, Swamp					
St. John's-Wort					
Sarsaparilla					
Self-Heal					
Shinleaf					
Shinleaf, Green					
Showy Orchis					
Silverweed					
Skullcap, Common					

Observer's List (cont.)	seen by			date	location
Skunk Cabbage					
Sleepy Catchfly					
Snakeroot, Black					
Snakeroot, White					
Solomon's Seal, False					
Solomon's Seal, Great					
Solomon's Seal, Hairy					
Solomon's Seal, Starry False					
Sowthistle, Smooth					
Spearmint					
Speedwell, Common					
Spring Beauty					
Spring Beauty, Broadleaf					
Spurge, Cypress					
Spurge, Flowering					
Spurge, Leafy					
Squawroot					
Squirrel Corn					
Starflower					
Starwort					
Stitchwort, Lesser					
Strawberry, Wild					
Strawberry, Woodland					
Sundew, Round-Leaved					
Sunflower, Tall					
Sunflower, Woodland					
Swamp Candle					
Sweet Cicely					
Tansy, Common					
Tansy, Huron					
Teasel					
Thimbleberry					
Thistle, Bull					
Thistle, Canada					
Thistle, Marsh					

Observer's List (cont.)	seen by			date	location
Thistle, Pitcher's					
Thistle, Spotted Star					
Thyme, Wild					
Tick-Trefoil, Pointed Leaved					
Toadflax, Bastard					
Toothwort, Broadleaf					
Toothwort, Cutleaf					
Trillium					
Trillium, Nodding					
Trillium, Red					
Turtlehead					
Twayblade, Heartleaf					
Twinflower					
Twisted Stalk, Rose					
Twisted Stalk, White					
Vervain, Blue					
Vetch, Crown					
Vetch, Hairy					
Violet, Bird-Foot					
Violet, Canada					
Violet, Common Blue					
Violet, Downy Yellow					
Violet, Smooth Yellow					
Virgin's Bower					
Water Arum					
Water-Hemlock					
Waterleaf, Virginia					
Water Lily, White					
Windflower, Red					
Wintergreen					
Woodnymph					
Wood-Sorrel, Yellow					
Wormwood, Tall					
Yarrow					
Yellow Rocket					

Wildflower Trails

Featured are eight Michigan trails selected for the following reasons:

· They are on lands that will continue to be accessible to the public.
· Together, they represent the various habitats found in Michigan, including meadows, woodlands, dunes, wetlands, and roadsides.
· The abundance of wildflowers found on these trails, as well as the number of different species, make them especially worthwhile.

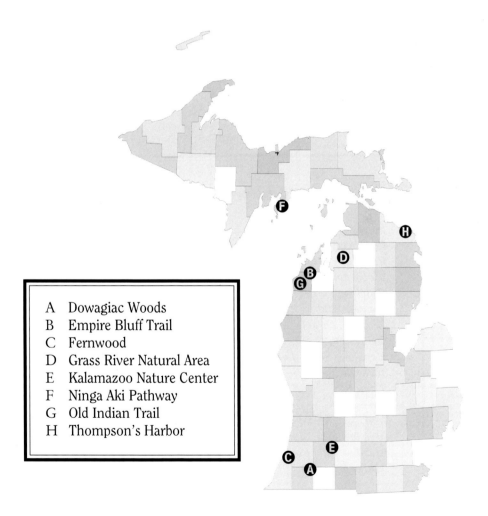

A   Dowagiac Woods
B   Empire Bluff Trail
C   Fernwood
D   Grass River Natural Area
E   Kalamazoo Nature Center
F   Ninga Aki Pathway
G   Old Indian Trail
H   Thompson's Harbor

DOWAGIAC WOODS NATURE SANCTUARY
(Cass County)

Located in southwestern Michigan near Dowagiac, this sanctuary is owned by the Michigan Nature Association and maintained by its members.

The 222 acres of the sanctuary exhibit not only a wide variety of species, but also spectacular views of large patches of single species.

Of the species found here, pay particular attention to Blue-Eyed Mary, Jacob's Ladder, Skunk Cabbage, Wood Anemone, Rue Anemone, False Rue Anemone, Wild Ginger, and Showy Orchis.

However, don't overlook any of the following if they are in bloom.

Wildflowers to See

Baneberry, Red	*Mayflower, Canada*
Baneberry, White	*Orchis, Showy*
Bedstraw, Yellow	*Ragwort, Golden*
Bloodroot	*Sweet Cicely*
Dutchman's Breeeches	*Spring Beauty*
Ginger, Wild	*Spring Beauty, Broadleaf*
Ginseng, Dwarf	*Squirrel Corn*
Geranium, Wild	*Toothwort, Broadleaf*
Hepatica, Sharp Lobed	*Toothwort, Cutleaf*
Jack-in-the-Pulpit	*Trillium, Large Flowered*
Trout Lily	*Trillium, Nodding*
Leek, Wild	*Violet, Canada*
Marigold, Marsh	*Violet, Common Blue*
Meadow Rue, Marsh	*Violet, Downy Yellow*
Meadow Rue, Early	*Waterleaf*
Mitrewort	

To Get There:

From the junction of M-62 and M-51 at the west edge of Dowagiac, travel 4 miles southwest on M-51 to Peavine Road, then a short distance west to California Road; go north on this road about 1¼ miles to Frost Road, then 6/10th of a mile to Dowagiac Woods parking area. Here pick up a brochure that gives information about the trails.

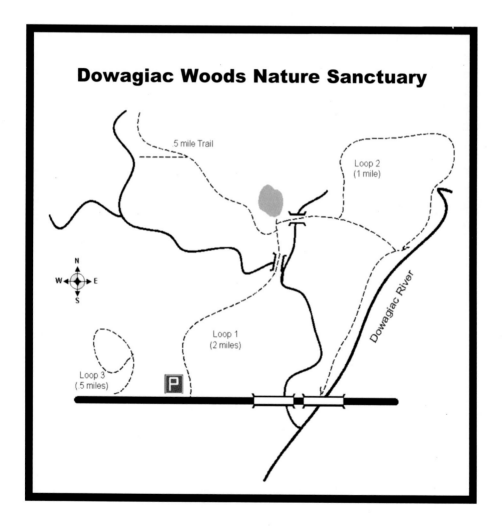

EMPIRE BLUFF TRAIL
(Benzie County)

Located south of Empire within the Sleeping Bear Dunes National Lakeshore is this wildflower trail with its spectacular views of Empire, the sand dunes, and Lake Michigan.

The trailhead is both the beginning and the end for the ¾-mile, well-defined trail. Along its length there are some fifty species of wildflowers. This trail leads through a variety of ecological zones, beginning in a meadow with wildflowers typical of a meadow zone. Next comes a woodland zone of beech and sugar maple. Being in a wooded area, most of the wildflowers here bloom in the spring before the tree leaves develop, shading the ground. Yet there are always wildflowers of some kind visible along this section of the trail, even in summer. Next, the trail crosses an old, abandoned orchard that most closely resembles a meadow zone at its present stage of ecological progression. After another pass through a wooded area, the trail comes out on the sandy bluffs of Lake Michigan, where flowers such as Dune Lily and Wormwood are apparent.

An interesting sight from these bluffs is the view in the distance of the original "Sleeping Bear," now eroded and windblown to a large, bearless, sandy pit. Picnic table and toilet are at the trailhead. There is no camping here but nearby areas in the park have well developed campgrounds.

Wildflowers to See

Bellwort	Herb Robert
Bloodroot	Jack-in-the-Pulpit
Blue Cohosh	Orange Hawkweed
Canada Mayflower	Partridgeberry
Canada Violet	Sharp-Lobed Hepatica
Columbine	Toothwort
Dune Lily	Spring Beauty
Dutchman's Breeches	Squawroot
Early Meadow-Rue	Squirrel Corn
Enchanter's Nighshade	Sweet Cicely
False Solomon's Seal	Trillium
Goat's-Beard	Virginia Waterleaf
Hairy Solomon's Seal	Yellow Trout Lily
Harebell	Yellow Violet

To Get There:

From the stoplight in the Village of Empire (¼ mile west of Visitor Center of Sleeping Bear Dunes National Lakeshore) go 1½ miles south on M-22 to Wilco Road, then ½ mile on Wilco to Trailhead.

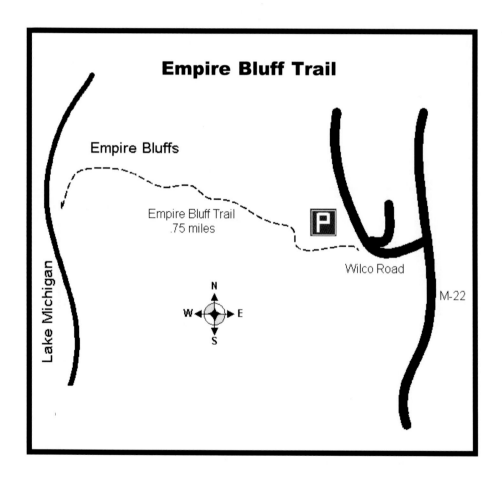

FERNWOOD NATURE CENTER AND BOTANIC GARDENS
(Berrien County)

Much more than a wildflower trail, Fernwood can best be referred to by its full name, Fernwood Nature Center and Botanic Gardens. The name most commonly used is simply "Fernwood."

Fernwood is a complete nature experience, but this book will confine itself to the wildflowers and what a visitor needs to know. All visitors must register at the Meeting House before entering the trails. Food and restrooms are available on the grounds. Many plants are labeled for identification, and explanatory information and maps are available at the Gift Shop. A small fee is charged to enter the grounds. Fernwood is open Tuesday through Sunday from 10 A.M. to 6 P.M. (April through September), 10 A.M. to 5 P.M. (October through March). Tea Room Lunches are served Tuesday through Friday from 11:30 to 2:00.

Wildflowers to See in May

Anemone, Rue	*Lady's-Slipper*
Anemone, False Rue	*May Apple*
Buttercup	*Phlox, Wood*
Bloodroot	*Poppy, Celandine*
Bluebells	*Spring Beauty*
Sweet Cicely	*Squirrel Corn*
Cowslip	*Solomon's Seal, Starry False*
Dutchman's Breeches	*Toothwort, Cutleaf*
Foamflower	*Trillium, Large Flowered*
Ginger, Wild	*Trillium, Nodding*
Hepatica, Sharp Lobed	*Trillium, Toad*
Hepatica, Round Lobed	*Twinleaf*
Jack-in-the-Pulpit	*Violet, Canada*

To Get There:

From Interstate 80/90 or US 12, take US 31 Bypass north to Walton Road. Go west on Walton Road to Range Line Road and go north on Range Line Road. Located at 13988 Range Line Road in Niles. Phone: (616) 695-6491

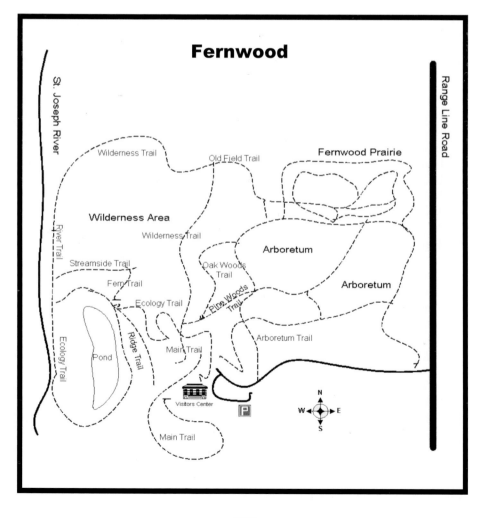

Ⓓ

GRASS RIVER NATURAL AREA
(Antrim County)

Located in west-central Antrim County, this trail offers over 1000 acres of a wide range of habitats, from dry uplands to river bottom swales. The area is owned by Antrim County. Trails are open dawn to dusk and a naturalist is available seven days a week, mid-June through Labor Day.

From parking area follow signs to Cabin (Interpretive Center); from here are four accessible boardwalk loops, one of which will accommodate wheelchairs. Identification labels for plants are found along each trail, with numbers that correspond to numbers in the trail guide. An upland trail can be reached from the Interpretive Center. Get information on how to find it at the center. Maps, books, and guides, as well as drinking water and toilet facilities are available here. Camping is not permitted.

Wildflowers to See

Agrimony	*Dock, Curled*	*Joe-Pye Weed*
Alyssum, Hoary	*Dogbane, Spreading*	*Ladies'-Tresses, Nodding*
Arbutus, Trailing	*Dwarf Cornell*	*Lady's-Slipper, Showy*
Arethusa	*Everlasting Pea*	*Lady's-Slipper, Yellow*
Arrow-Grass, Seaside	*Forget-Me-Not*	*Lily-of-the-Valley, Wild*
Basil, Wild	*Gaywings*	*Loosestrife, Tufted*
Black-Eyed Susan	*Gentian, Spurred*	*Marigold, Marsh*
Blue Flag	*Ginseng, Dwarf*	*Meadow-Rue, Early*
Boneset	*Goat's -Beard, Yellow*	*Milkweed*
Buckbean	*Goldenrod, Canada*	*Mitrewort, Naked*
Buttercup	*Goldthread*	*Moneywort*
Cardinal-Flower	*Grass Pink*	*Mullein*
Cattail	*Grass-of-Parnassus*	*Orchid, Purple Fringed*
Cinquefoil, Marsh	*Great Lobelia*	*Orchid,*
Cinquefoil,	*Hawkweed, Orange*	*Tall Northern Bog*
Rough-Fruited	*Hawkweed, Yellow*	*Partridgeberry*
Clover, Red	*Heartleaf Twayblade*	*Peppermint*
Columbine	*Herb-Robert*	*Pinesap*
Coneflower,	*Horsemint*	*Pitcher Plant*
Green-Headed	*Indian Paintbrush*	*Prince's Pine*
Cranberry	*Indian Pipe*	*Queen Anne's Lace*
Cucumber-Root, Indian	*Jack-in-the-Pulpit*	*Rose, Swamp*
Dandelion	*Jewelweed, Spotted*	*St. John's Wort*

Sarsaparilla, Wild
Shinleaf
Silverweed
Skullcap
Solomon's Seal,
  False
Solomon's Seal,
  Starry False
Starflower
Strawberry

Sundew,
  Round-Leaved
Thistle, Marsh
Toothwort
Trillium
Trillium, Nodding
Turtlehead
Twinflower
Vetch, Crown
Violet, Blue

Violet, Downy Yellow
Virgin's Bower
Water-Horehound,
  Cut-Leaved
Wintercress
Wintergreen
Wood-Sorrel, Yellow
Wormwood
Yarrow

To Get There:

From Alden go north on East Torch Lake Road. About one mile north the road bears to the left. Go straight here and at the top of the hill follow Alden Highway to Grass River Natural Area sign on left side of road (about 4 miles). Follow two-track road to parking area (1.8 miles).

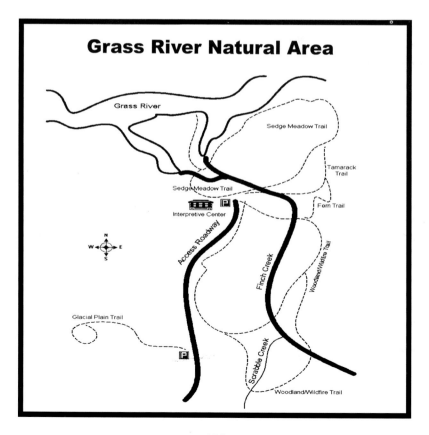

Grass River Natural Area

KALAMAZOO NATURE CENTER
(Kalamazoo County)

Located on the north edge of the city of Kalamazoo, this nature center has been selected because of the many educational exhibits as well as its wildflower trails. There is an area devoted to prairie flowers that usually are not found on most other wildflower trails in Michigan.

Because much of the trail system is through wooded areas, it is best to visit the center in early spring before many of the tree leaves are fully developed and shade out the vegetation below. Early April to the middle of May is optimal. However, any visit to the center offers interesting sights.

In the early spring expect to see Narrow Leaf Spring Beauty, Hepatica, and Harbinger of Spring among many others. Later in the season a wide variety of southern Michigan wildflowers are in bloom.

Upon your arrival, be sure to visit the Interpretive Center, where maps and nature related information are available.

Wildflowers to See

Anemone, False Rue	Lily, Trout
Anemone, Wood	Marigold, Marsh
Bellwort, Large-Flowered	May Apple
Bishop's Cap	Skunk Cabbage
Bloodroot	Solomon's Seal, False
Blue-Eyed Mary	Solomon's Seal, Hairy
Cicely, Sweet	Spring Beauty, Narrow Leaf
Cohosh, Blue	Squirrel Corn
Dutchman's Breeches	Toothwort, Cut-Leaved
Ginger, Wild	Trillium
Harbinger of Spring	Violet, Canada
Hepatica, Sharp-Lobed	Violet, Common Blue
Jack-in-the-Pulpit	Violet, Downy Yellow

To Get There:

From downtown Kalamazoo follow Westnedge Avenue north. The Nature Center entrance is at 7000 Westnedge and is well marked.

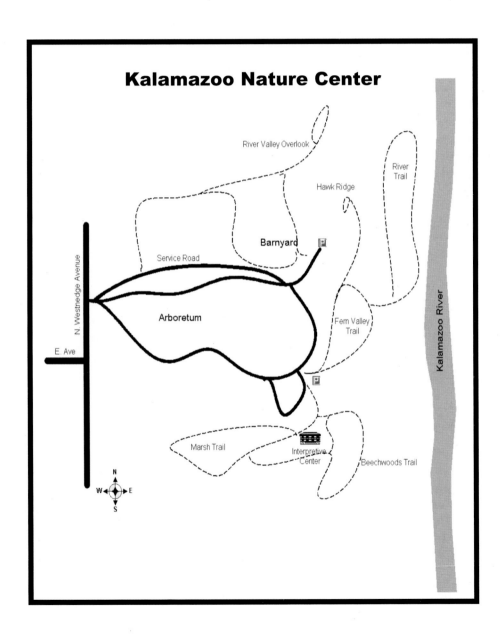

NINGA AKI (MOTHER EARTH) PATHWAY
Portage Bay State Forest Campground
(Delta County)

It might be a long way to the Garden Peninsula, located 16 miles west of Manistique on the north shore of Lake Michigan; however, you will find the trip rewarding when you experience the variety of wildflowers.

Wildflowers: From the time you turn onto "LL" Road and all the way to the campground, be looking for flowers on the sides of the road. Depending on the time of year, expect to see such flowers as Yellow Lady's Slippers, Columbine, Indian Paintbrush, Wild Rose, and Wood Lily. As for the trails, the Bog Lake is the shorter; Ninga Aki (Mother Earth) trail is longer but here the Dwarf Lake Iris, a Threatened Species, is visible. Please stay on the trail through the patches of iris. This trail comes out on the lakeshore and, in general, follows it back to the trailhead. Along this part of the trail, be on the alert for another Threatened Species, Pitcher's Thistle.

Be sure to check the beach right at the campground, as many species are apparent here. This is also true of short spur roads leading to old borrow-pits and boat launches.

Toward the end of May look for these flowers along the road between Road 183 and the campground:

Blue-Eyed Grass
Buttercup
Clintonia
Columbine
Gaywings
Iris, Dwarf Lake
Lady's-Slipper
Mayflower, Canada
Paintbrush, Indian
Rock Cress, Lyre-Leaved
Sarsaparilla
Silverweed
Solomon's Seal, False
Solomon's Seal, Starry False
Violets

Wildflowers of Ninga Aki Pathway, beach, and side roads near the campground:

Arbutus
Aster, Large Leaf
Baneberry
Basil
Bearberry
Boneset
Buttercup
Cinquefoil
Clintonia
Columbine
Coralroot, Early
Cornel, Dwarf
Corydalis, Pale
Cowslip
Daisy, Ox-Eye
Dogbane

Wildflowers to See *(cont.)*

Fireweed	*Iris, Dwarf Lake*	*Mint, Wild*
Fleabane	*Iris, Tall Blue*	*Mitrewort, Naked*
Foamflower	*Jack-in-the-Pulpit*	*Mullein, Common*
Forget-Me-Not	*Lady's-Slipper*	*Paintbrush, Indian*
Gentian, Spur	*Lily, Wood*	*Plantain, Common*
Goldenrod	*Lobelia, Kalm*	*Polygala, Fringed*
Goldthread	*Thistle, Bull*	*Pyrola, Greenish*
Harebell	*Thimbleberry **	*Flowered*
Hawkweed, Field	*Thistle, Marsh*	*Primrose, Evening*
Hawkweed, Orange	*Thistle, Pitcher's*	*Primrose, Birdseye*
Hawkweed, Yellow	*Twinflower*	*Wormwood*
Heal-All	*Mayflower, Canada*	*Yarrow*
Horehound, Water	*Milkweed, Common*	** a shrub*

To Get There:

From the Manistique River Bridge at Manistique, go west on US-2 to Garden Corners (16 miles). Turn on to Road 183 and go through the Village of Garden. About 5 miles from Garden the road makes a sharp turn to the right. At this corner is a sign that says "State Forest Campground." Make a jog to the left on "LL" road, and travel south about 2 miles to a road on the left. A sign here also says "State Forest Campground." You are now 5 miles from the campground which, when you reach it, has a sign, "Portage Bay Campground." Go straight ahead .6 miles to trailhead.

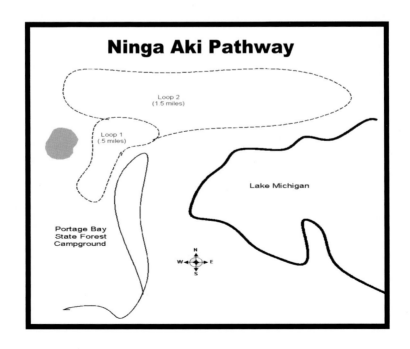

Ninga Aki Pathway

Loop 2
(1.5 miles)

Loop 1
(.5 miles)

Lake Michigan

Portage Bay
State Forest
Campground

Ⓖ

OLD INDIAN TRAIL
(Benzie County)

Located south of Sleeping Bear Sand Dunes, this well-maintained trail crosses undulating terrain with no long or steep climbs. The trail is mostly shaded by mixed hardwoods and conifers. Because of the shade, wildflowers are best observed in the spring and early summer. A main attraction on this trail is the Cardinal-Flower, which blooms from late July into early September. It occurs in a wet area about ½ mile from the trailhead on the most northern section of the trail system.

Farther along the trail makes a sharp turn to the left. At this point a spur trail goes to the right and leads to Lake Michigan with its sandy beach and view of the sand dunes.

There is a pit toilet at the trailhead but no water. Camping is not permitted. An excellent campground can be found 3.8 miles north on M-22.

Wildflowers to See

Arbutus	Goatsbeard	St. John's Wort
Arabis	Goldenrod	Solomon's Seal,
Aster, Large Leaf	Herb Robert	Starry False
Aster, Small White	Hawkweed	Solomon's Seal,
Arum, Water	Heal-All	Great
Basil	Horehound,	Sarsaparilla
Bearberry	Cut-Leaf Water	Starflower
Bedstraw	Iris, Blue	Strawberry, Wild
Betony, Wood	Jack-in-the-Pulpit	Speedwell, Common
Campion, Bladder	Knapweed, Spotted	Toadflax, Bastard
Cardinal -Flower	Lettuce, White	Twinflower
Carrot, Wild	Mayflower, Canada	Thistle, Pitcher's
Cicely, Sweet	Mint, Wild	Trillium
Cucumber-Root,	Moccasin Flower	Violet, Long-Spurred
Indian	Mullein, Common	Wintergreen
Columbine	Partridge Berry	Wormwood, Tall
Daisy, Ox-Eye	Parsnip, Water	Yarrow
Cornel, Dwarf	Primrose, Evening	
Gaywings	Puccoon, Hairy	

To Get There:

From the traffic light at Empire, travel south 13 miles on M-22 to trailhead. Or, from Frankfort, go north approximately 8 miles on M-22 to Sutter Road; continue on M-22 a few hundred feet to trailhead on the left side of the road.

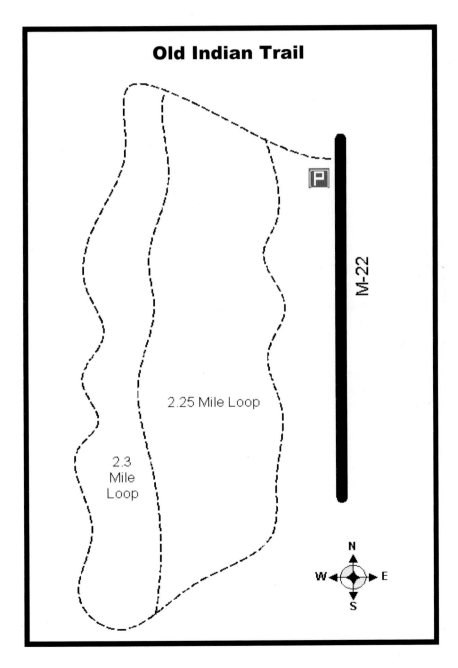

Old Indian Trail

2.25 Mile Loop

2.3 Mile Loop

M-22

P

N
W E
S

THOMPSON'S HARBOR STATE PARK
(Presque Isle County)

One of Michigan's newest state parks is located in Presque Isle County. Because of its newness and lack of development, there is only one road open to the public. This lack of development means the vegetation has only been slightly disturbed, a plus for the wildflower seeker.

Although this is a state park, there are no picnic tables or drinking water. Camping is not permitted. There is a clean, well-maintained toilet at the trailhead. There are rumors of rattlesnakes in the area, but by observing reasonable caution and staying on the trail there should be no problem.

The trailhead sign divides the trail into three loops. It might be possible to work both Loops #1 and #2 the same day. To try to do the three loops at one time would involve walking more than six miles and might not leave time to see the flowers.

A suggested route is to follow Loop #1 and come back to where Loop #2 takes off from Loop #1. At this point a decision can be made as to whether to stay on Loop #1 back to the parking area, or to follow Loop #2 to the same destination.

Wildflowers to See

Aster, Large Leaf	Primrose, Birdseye
Bearberry	Sarsaparilla, Wild
Betony, Wood	Snakeroot, Seneca
Bunchberry	Silverweed
Columbine	Solomon's Seal
Coral Root, Striped	Solomon's Seal,
Gaywings	Starry False
Gentian, Fringed	Strawberry, Wild
Iris, Dwarf Lake	Lady's-Slipper, Yellow
Lily, Dune	Sundew, Round Leaf
Mayflower, Canada	Toadflax
Mullein, Common	Twin Flower
Pitcher Plant	Violet, Blue Marsh

To Get There:

If coming from the northwest:

From the junction of M-65 north and US-23, go south on US-23 4.9 miles to park entrance.

If coming from the south or Alpena:

At the junction of US-23 and M-32 (in downtown Alpena) travel north on US-23 twenty-five miles to state park.

Caution: Do not park at the entrance sign. Continue another 1½ miles into the park, following the trailhead signs to a parking area where the trails begin.

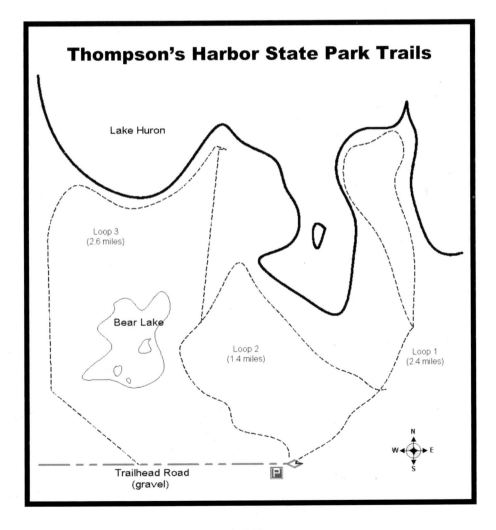

Thompson's Harbor State Park Trails

Lake Huron

Loop 3
(2.6 miles)

Bear Lake

Loop 2
(1.4 miles)

Loop 1
(2.4 miles)

Trailhead Road
(gravel)

Index

A

Aaron's Rod   68
Achillea millefolium   52
Actaea alba   40
Actaea rubra   40
Adder's Tongue   54
Agrimonia gryposepala   66
Agrimony   66
Agrostemma githago   86
Alyssum, Hoary   44
Ambrosia artemisiifolia   108
Anaphalis margaritacea   42
Anemone, Canada   28
Anemone canadensis   28
Anemone, False Rue   30
Anemone multifida   72
Anemone quinquefolia   28
Anemone, Rue   30
Anemone, Wood   28
Anemonella thalictroides   30
Anthemis cotula   38
Apios americana   106
Apocynum androsaemifolium   84
Aquilegia canadensis   72
Arabis lyrata   32
Aralia hispida   32
Aralia nudicaulis   32
Arbutus, Trailing   28
Arctium lappa   94
Arctium minus   94
Arctostaphylos uva-ursi   34
Arenaria stricta   38
Arethusa   74
Arethusa bulbosa   74
Arisaema triphyllum   90
Arrow-Grass, Seaside   106
Artemisia campestris   108
Asarum canadense   90
Asclepias incarnata   84
Asclepias syriaca   84
Asclepias tuberosa   62
Asphodel, Sticky False   36
Aster, Flat-Topped   52
Aster laevis   94
Aster, Large-Leaved   94
Aster macrophyllus   94
Aster, New England   94
Aster novae-angliae   94
Aster, Smooth   94
Aster umbellatus   52

B

Balsam-Apple   52
Baneberry, Red   40
Baneberry, White   40
Baptisia leucantha   38
Barbarea vulgaris   60
Basil, Wild   82
Beach Pea   80
Bearberry   34
Beard-Tongue, Hairy   96

Bellwort, Large-Flowered   54
Bergamot, Wild   82
Berteroa incana   44
Betony, Wood   58
Bindweed, Field   44
Bird-Foot Violet   90
Birdseye Primrose   28
Birdsfoot Trefoil   68
Bishop's Cap   24
Black-Eyed Susan   64
Blazing Star, Rough   94
Bloodroot   26
Blue Flag   100
Blue Sailors   104
Blue-Eyed Grass   100
Blue-Eyed Mary   98
Bluebell   102
Blueweed   102
Boneset   50
Bouncing Bet   86
Broom-Rape, Clustered   34
Buckbean   34
Bugloss, Viper's   102
Bull Thistle   88
Bullhead Lily   66
Bunchberry   28
Burdock, Common   94
Butter-and-Eggs   68
Buttercup   54, 55
Butterfly Weed   62
Butterwort   92

C

Calla palustris   28
Calla, Wild   28
Calopogon pulchellus   78
Caltha palustris   54
Calypso   74
Calypso bulbosa   74
Campanula rotundifolia   102
Campion, Bladder   36
Campion, White   50
Cardamine bulbosa   24
Cardinal-Flower   88
Carrot, Wild   44
Castilleja coccinea   72
Castilleja septentrionalis   48
Catchfly, Sleepy   86
Catmint   32
Catnip   32
Cattail   106
Caulophyllum thalictroides   90
Centaurea jacea   88
Centaurea maculosa   88
Chamomile, Scentless   38
Chamomile, Stinking   38
Checkerberry   46
Chelone glabra   48
Cherry, ground   68
Chicory   104
Chimaphila umbellata   80
Chrysanthemum leucanthemum   42
Cicely, Sweet   30
Cichorium intybus   104

Cicuta maculata   44
Cinquefoil, Marsh   96
Cinquefoil, Rough-Fruited   64
Cinquefoil, Sulfur   64
Cinquefoil, Three-Toothed   36
Circaea quadrisulcata   34
Cirsium arvense   88
Cirsium palustre   96
Cirsium pitcheri   32
Cirsium vulgare   88
Claytonia caroliniana   72
Claytonia virginica   72
Clematis virginiana   52
Clintonia borealis   54
Clover, Red   80
Clustered Broom-Rape   34
Cockle, Corn or Purple   86
Cohosh, Blue   90
Collinsia verna   98
Columbine   72
Comandra livida   40
Comandra, Northern   40
Comandra umbellata   40
Coneflower   64
Coneflower, Green-Headed   70
Coneflower, Tall   70
Conopholis americana   58
Convolvulus arvensis   44
Coptis trifolia   24
Corallorhiza maculata   92
Corallorhiza striata   92
Corallorhiza trifida   92
Coralroot, Northern or Early 92
Coralroot, Spotted   92
Coralroot, Striped   92
Coreopsis   56
Coreopsis lanceolata   56
Cornus canadensis   28
Coronilla varia   80
Corydalis, Pale   76
Corydalis sempervirens   76
Cow Parsnip   44
Cow Wheat   48
Cowslip   54
Cranberry, Large   80
Cranberry, Small   80
Cranesbill, Spotted   76
Cress, Lyre-Leaved Rock   32
Cress, Spring   24
Crown Vetch   80
Cucumber, Wild   52
Cucumber-Root, Indian   54
Culver's Root   48
Cynoglossum officinale   92
Cypripedium acaule   74
Cypripedium arietinum   74
Cypripedium calceolus   58
Cypripedium reginae   78

D

Daisy, Ox-Eye   42
Dame's Rocket   82
Dandelion, Common   56
Daucus carota   44
Day Lily   62

Death Camas 44
Dentaria diphylla 24
Dentaria laciniata 24
Deptford Pink 86
Desmodium glutinosum 96
Devil's Paintbrush 64
Dicentra canadensis 26
Dicentra cucullaria 26
Dianthus armeria 86
Dipsacus sylvestris 84
Dock, Curled or Sour 106
Dogbane, Spreading 84
Dogfennel 38
Dogmint 82
Doll's-Eyes 40
Dragon's Mouth 74
Drosera rotundifolia 50
Dutchman's Breeches 26
Dwarf Cornel 28

E

Echinocystis lobata 52
Echium vulgare 102
Enchanter's Nightshade 34
Epigaea repens 28
Epilobium angustifolium 84
Epipactis helleborine 108
Erigeron strigosus 36
Erythronium albidum 54
Erythronium americanum 54
Eupatorium maculatum 88
Eupatorium perfoliatum 50
Eupatorium rugosum 42
Euphorbia corolatta 32
Euphorbia cyparissias 108
Euphorbia esula 62
Evening Lychnis 50
Evening Primrose 66
Everlasting Pea 78
Everlasting, Pearly 42

F

Fairy Slipper 74
Fawn Lily 54
Fireweed 84
Flat-Topped Aster 52
Fleabane 36
Foamflower 26
Forget-Me-Not 102
Fragaria vesca 36
Fragaria virginiana 36

G

Gaultheria procumbens 46
Gaywings 78
Gentian, Bottle or Closed 104
Gentian, Fringed 104
Gentian, Spurred 106
Gentiana andrewsii 104
Gentiana crinita 104
Geranium maculatum 76
Geranium robertianum 76
Geranium, Wild 76
Ginger, Wild 90
Ginseng, Dwarf 32

Goat's Rue 56
Goat's-Beard 62
Golden Alexanders 60
Golden Ragwort 56
Goldenrod, Bluestem 70
Goldenrod, Canada 70
Goldthread 24
Grass Pink 78
Grass-of-Parnassus 52
Grass-of-Parnassus, Small 52
Great Lobelia 104
Great Willow Herb 84
Greenbrier 34
Ground Cherry 68
Ground Nut 106

H

Habenaria hyperborea 108
Habenaria psycodes 98
Halenia deflexa 106
Harebell 102
Hawkweed, Field or Yellow 60
Hawkweed, Orange 64
Hawkweed, Smoothish 60
Heal-All 92
Heartleaf Twayblade 108
Heather, False 58
Helianthus divaricatus 70
Helianthus giganteus 70
Helleborine 108
Hemlock, Water 44
Hepatica acutiloba 72
Hepatica americana 72
Hepatica, Round-Lobed 72
Hepatica, Sharp-Lobed 72
Heracleum lanatum 44
Herb-Robert 76
Hemerocallis fulva 62
Hesperis matronalis 82
Hieracium aurantiacum 64
Hieracium florentinum 60
Hieracium floribundum 60
Hieracium pratense 60
Honesty 82
Horehound, Cut-Leaved Water
  50
Horsemint 68
Hound's Tongue 92
Hudsonia tomentosa 58
Hydrophyllum virginianum 92
Hypericum perforatum 66

I

Impatiens biflora 64
Indian Cucumber-Root 54
Indian Paintbrush 72
Indian Pipe 48
Indian Potato 106
Indian Turnip 90
Indigo, Prairie False 38
Indigo, White False 38
Iris, Blue 100
Iris, Dwarf Lake 100
Iris lacustris 100
Iris versicolor 100
Ivy, Poison 48

Ivy, Three-Leaved 48

J

Jack-in-the-Pulpit 90
Jewelweed, Spotted 64
Joe-Pye Weed 88

K

King Devil 60
Kinnikinick 34
Knapweed, Brown 88
Knapweed, Spotted 88

L

Ladies' Tresses, Common 50
Ladies' Tresses, Nodding 50
Lady's-Slipper, Pink 74
Lady's-Slipper, Ram's-Head 74
Lady's-Slipper, Showy 78
Lady's-Slipper, Yellow 58
Lathyrus latifolius 78
Lathyrus maritimus 80
Leonurus cardiaca 98
Lesser Stitchwort 34
Lettuce, White 52
Liatris aspera 94
Lilium philadelphicum 62
Lilium superbum 62
Lily, Bluebead 54
Lily, Bullhead 66
Lily, Day 62
Lily, Dune 44
Lily, Fawn 54
Lily, Michigan 62
Lily, Tuberous Water 50
Lily, White Water 50
Lily, Wood 62
Lily, Yellow Trout 54
Lily-of-the-Valley, Wild 26
Linaria vulgaris 68
Linnaea borealis 78
Listera cordata 108
Lithospermum canescens 58
Lithospermum caroliniense 58
Liverleaf 72
Lobelia cardinalis 88
Lobelia, Great 104
Lobelia siphilitica 104
Loosestrife, Purple or Spiked 96
Loosestrife, Tufted 56
Loosestrife, Yellow 66
Lotus corniculatus 68
Lousewort 58
Lunaria annua 82
Lupine 100
Lupine, Garden 100
Lupinus perennis 100
Lupinus polyphylus 100
Lychnis alba 50
Lychnis coronaria 86
Lychnis, Evening 50
Lycopus americanus 50
Lyre-Leaved Rock Cress 32
Lysimachia nummularia 64

Lysimachia terrestris 66
Lysimachia thyrsiflora 56
Lythrum salicaria 96

M

Maianthemum canadense 26
Mallow, Musk 82
Malva moschata 82
Mandarin, Rose 76
Mandrake 30
Marguerite 42
Marigold, Marsh 54
Matricaria maritima 38
May Apple 30
Mayflower, Canada 26
Meadow Rose 86
Meadow-Rue, Early 42
Meadow-Rue, Purple 42
Meadowsweet 40
Medeola virginiana 54
Melampyrum lineare 48
Mentha arvensis 98
Mentha piperita 98
Mentha spicata 98
Menyanthes trifoliata 34
Milkweed, Common 84
Milkweed, Orange 62
Milkweed, Swamp 84
Milkwort, Field 84
Milkwort, Racemed 78
Mimulus ringens 96
Mint, Wild 98
Mitchella repens 42
Mitella diphylla 24
Mitella nuda 24
Mitrewort 24
Mitrewort, False 26
Mitrewort, Naked 24
Moccasin Flower 74
Monarda fistulosa 82
Monarda punctata 68
Moneses uniflora 46
Money Plant 82
Moneywort 64
Monkey Flower, Square-
 Stemmed 96
Monotropa hypopithys 68
Monotropa uniflora 48
Moonwort 82
Motherwort 98
Mullein, Common 68
Mullein, Moth 40
Mullein-Pink 86
Musk Mallow 82
Myosotis scorpioides 102
Myrtle 102

N

Nepeta cataria 32
New England Aster 94
Nightshade 96
Nightshade, Enchanter's 34
Nodding Ladies' Tresses 50
Nodding Trillium 30
Nuphar variegatum 66
Nymphaea tuberosa 50

O

Oenothera biennis 66
Old Man's Beard 52
One-Flowered Wintergreen 46
One-Sided Shinleaf 46
Orchid, Purple Fringed 98
Orchid, Tall Northern Bog 108
Orchis, Showy 74
Orchis spectabilis 74
Orobanche fasciculata 34
Osmorhiza claytoni 30
Ox-Eye Daisy 42
Oxalis stricta 58
Oyster Plant 62

P

Painted Cup 72
Painted Cup, Pale 48
Panax trifolium 32
Papoose-Root 90
Parnassia glauca 52
Parnassia parviflora 52
Parsnip, Cow 44
Parsnip, Water 46
Parsnip, Wild 60
Partridgeberry 42
Pastinaca sativa 60
Pea, Beach 80
Pea, Everlasting 78
Pearly Everlasting 42
Pedicularis canadensis 58
Penstemon hirsutus 96
Peppermint 98
Pepperwort 24
Periwinkle 102
Phlox divaricata 90
Phlox, Wood 90
Physalis heterophylla 68
Pickerelweed 102
Pimpernel, Yellow 60
Pinesap 68
Pinguicula vulgaris 92
Pink, Deptford 86
Pink, Grass 78
Pipsissewa 80
Pitcher Plant 76
Pitcher's Thistle 32
Podophyllum peltatum 30
Pogonia ophioglossoides 74
Pogonia, Rose 74
Poison Ivy 48
Polygala, Fringed 78
Polygala paucifolia 78
Polygala polygama 78
Polygala sanguinea 84
Polygonatum canaliculatum 38
Polygonatum pubescens 38
Pondlily, Bullhead or Yellow 66
Pontederia cordata 102
Potato, Indian 106
Potentilla anserina 64
Potentilla palustris 96
Potentilla recta 64
Potentilla tridentata 36
Prairie Indigo 38

Prenanthes alba 52
Primrose, Birdseye 28
Primrose, Evening 66
Primula mistassinica 28
Prince's Pine 80
Prunella vulgaris 92
Puccoon, Hairy 58
Puccoon, Hoary 58
Pyrola asarifolia 80
Pyrola elliptica 46
Pyrola, Pink 80
Pyrola secunda 46
Pyrola virens 46

Q

Queen Anne's Lace 44

R

Rabbit Pea 56
Ragweed 108
Ragwort, Golden 56
Ranunculus acris 54
Red Robin 76
Rhus radicans 48
Rock Bells 72
Rock Cress, Lyre-Leaved 32
Rock Sandwort 38
Rocket, Dame's or Sweet 82
Rocket, Yellow 60
Rosa blanda 86
Rosa palustris 86
Rose Mandarin 76
Rose, Meadow 86
Rose Pogonia 74
Rose, Smooth 86
Rose, Swamp 86
Rose Twisted Stalk 76
Rough Blazing Star 94
Rough-Fruited Cinquefoil 64
Round-Leaved Sundew 50
Round-Lobe Hepatica 72
Rubus parviflorus 40
Rudbeckia hirta 64
Rudbeckia laciniata 70
Rue Anemone 30
Rumex crispus 106

S

St. John's-Wort 66
Sandwort, Rock 38
Sanguinara canadensis 26
Sanicula marilandica 36
Saponaria officinalis 86
Sarracenia purpurea 76
Sarsaparilla 32
Sarsaparilla, Bristly 32
Satureja vulgaris 82
Scutellaria galericulata 104
Self-Heal 92
Senecio aureus 56
Shinleaf 46
Shinleaf, Green 46
Shinleaf, One-Sided 46
Showy Lady's-Slipper 78
Showy Orchis 74

Sidebells 46
Silene antirrhina 86
Silene cucubalus 36
Silkweed 84
Silverweed 64
Sisyrinchium albidum 100
Sium suave 46
Skullcap, Common 104
Skullcap, Marsh 104
Skunk Cabbage 106
Sleepy Catchfly 86
Smilacina racemosa 38
Smilacina stellata 38
Smilax hispida 34
Snakeroot, Black 36
Snakeroot, White 42
Soapwort 86
Solanum dulcamara 96
Solidago caesia 70
Solidago canadensis 70
Solomon's Seal, False 38
Solomon's Seal, Great 38
Solomon's Seal, Hairy 38
Solomon's Seal, Starry False 38
Sonchus uliginosus 66
Sorrel, Yellow Wood- 58
Sour Dock 106
Sowthistle, Smooth 66
Spearmint 98
Speedwell, Common 102
Spiked Loosestrife 96
Spiranthes cernua 50
Spirea alba 40
Spreading Dogbane 84
Spring Beauty 72
Spring Beauty, Broadleaf 72
Spring Cress 24
Spurge, Cypress 108
Spurge, Flowering 32
Spurge, Leafy 62
Spurred Gentian 106
Square-Stemmed Monkey
   Flower 96
Squawroot 58
Squirrel Corn 26
Star Thistle, Spotted 88
Starflower 26
Starwort 34
Stellaria graminea 34
Stellaria longipes 34
Stinking Benjamin 76
Stitchwort, Lesser 34
Strawberry, Wild 36
Strawberry, Woodland 36
Streptopus amplexifolius 76
Streptopus roseus 76
Sundew, Round-Leaved 50
Sunflower, Tall 70
Sunflower, Woodland 70
Swamp Candle 66
Swamp Milkweed 84
Swamp Rose 86
Sweet Cicely 30
Sweet Rocket 82
Symplocarpus foetidus 106

T

Taenidia integerrima 60
Tanacetum huronense 70
Tanacetum vulgare 70
Tansy, Common 70
Tansy, Huron 70
Taraxacum officinale 56
Teasel 84
Tephrosia virginiana 56
Thalictrum dasycarpum 42
Thalictrum dioicum 42
Thimbleberry 40
Thistle, Bull 88
Thistle, Canada 88
Thistle, Marsh 96
Thistle, Pitcher's 32
Thistle, Spotted Star 88
Thoroughwort 50
Three-Leaved Ivy 48
Three-Toothed Cinquefoil 36
Thyme, Wild 82
Thymus serpyllum 82
Tiarella cordifolia 26
Tick-Trefoil, Pointed Leaved
   94
Tickseed 56
Toadflax, Bastard 40
Tofieldia glutinosa 36
Toothwort, Broadleaf 24
Toothwort, Cutleaf 24
Touch-Me-Not 64
Tragopogon dubius 62
Trailing Arbutus 28
Trefoil, Birdsfoot 68
Trientalis borealis 26
Trifolium pratense 80
Triglochin maritima 106
Trillium 30
Trillium cernuum 30
Trillium erectum 76
Trillium grandiflorum 30
Trillium, Large-Flowered 30
Trillium, Nodding 30
Trillium, Red 76
Trout Lily, Yellow 54
Tuberous Water Lily 50
Turnip, Indian 90
Turtlehead 48
Twayblade, Heartleaf 108
Twinflower 78
Twisted Stalk, Rose 76
Twisted Stalk, White 76
Typha latifolia 106

U

Uvularia grandiflora 54

V

Vaccinium macrocarpon 80
Vaccinium oxycoccos 80
Verbascum blattaria 40
Verbascum thapsus 68
Verbena hastata 104

Veronica officinalis 102
Veronicastrum virginicum 48
Vervain, Blue 104
Vetch, Crown 80
Vetch, Hairy 90
Vicia villosa 90
Vinca minor 102
Viola canadensis 30
Viola eriocarpa 56
Viola papilionacea 100
Viola pedata 90
Viola pubescens 56
Violet, Bird-Foot 90
Violet, Canada 30
Violet, Common Blue 100
Violet, Downy Yellow 56
Violet, Smooth Yellow 56
Viper's Bugloss 102
Virginia Waterleaf 92
Virgin's Bower 52

W

Water Arum 28
Water Lily, Tuberous 50
Water Lily, White 50
Water-Hemlock 44
Water-Horehound, Cut-Leaved 50
Waterleaf, Virginia 92
Willow Herb, Great 84
Windflower, Red 72
Winter Cress 60
Wintergreen 46
Wintergreen, One-Flowered 46
Wood Betony 58
Wood-Sorrel, Yellow 58
Woodnymph 46
Wormwood, Tall 108

Y

Yarrow 52
Yellow Rocket 60

Z

Zizia aurea 60
Zygadenus glaucus 44

Bibliography

Angier, *Field Guide to Edible Wild Plants.* Stackpole Books, Harrisburg, PA.

Audubon Society. *Field Guide to North American Wildflowers, Eastern Region.* Alfred A. Knopf, New York, NY.

Case, Frederick, Jr. and Roberta B. *Trilliums.* Timber Press, Portland, OR.

Case, Frederick, Jr. *Orchids of the Great Lakes Region.* Cranbrook Institute of Science, Bloomfield Hills, MI.

Courtnay and Zimmerman. *Wildflowers and Weeds.* Van Nostrand Reinhold Co., Cincinnati, OH.

Embertson and Conrader. *Pods, Wildflowers and Weeds in Their Final Beauty.* Charles Scribner's Sons, New York, NY.

Gleason. *New Britton and Brown Illustrated Flora,* 3 volumes. Hafner Publishing Co., New York, NY.

Gleason and Cronquist. *Manual of Vascular Plants of Northeastern United States and Adjacent Canada.* Van Norstrand, New York, NY.

James, Wilma Roberts. *Know Your Poisonous Plants.* Naturegraph Publishers, Healdsburg, CA.

Janke, Robert. *Wildflowers of Isle Royale.* Isle Royale Natural History Assoc., Houghton, MI.

Moyle, J. and Moyle, W. *Northland Wildflowers, A Guide for the Minnesota Region.* University of Minnesota Press, Minneapolis, MN.

Naegele, Thomas A. *Edible and Medicinal Plants of the Great Lakes Region.* Wilderness Adventure Books, Chelsea, MI.

Newcomb, L. *Wildflower Guide.* Little, Brown, Boston, MA.

Peterson and McKenny. *Field Guide to Wildflowers.* Houghton Mifflin Co., Boston, MA.

Rickett, H.W. *Wildflowers of the United States, The Northeastern States,* 2 volumes. McGraw-Hill, New York, NY.

Simonds, Roberta. *Wildflowers of the Great Lakes States.* Stipes Publishng Co. Champaign, IL.

Smith, Helen. *Michigan Wildflowers.* Cranbrook Institute of Science, Bloomfield Hills, MI.

Stupka, A. *Wildflowers in Color.* Harper and Row, New York, NY.

Voss, Edward. *Michigan Flora,* 3 volumes. Cranbrook Institute of Science and University of Michigan Herbarium, Bloomfield Hills, MI.